Sly Fox

A COMEDY IN TWO ACTS
ADAPTED FROM VALPONE

by

Larry Gelbart

SAMUEL FRENCH

FOUNDED 1830

New York Hollywood London Toronto
SAMUELFRENCH.COM

OPENING NIGHT, DECEMBER 14, 1976

BROADHURST THEATRE

**SIR LEW GRADE, MARTIN STARGER AND
THE SHUBERT ORGANIZATION**

Present

GEORGE C. SCOTT

in

"SLY FOX"

by

LARRY GELBART

Based on Volpone by Ben Jonson

Directed by

ARTHUR PENN

Also starring

TRISH VAN DEVERE   JACK GILFORD
BOB DISHY   GRETCHEN WYLER
JOHN RAMSEY   JAMES GALLERY
JOHN HEFFERNAN

and

HECTOR ELIZONDO as ABLE

Production Designed and Lighted by   Costumes by
GEORGE JENKINS   **ALBERT WOLSKY**

The Producers and Theatre Management are Members
of The League of New York Theatres and Producers, Inc.

Julian Schlossberg   Roy Furman   Ben Sprecher
Michael Gardner   Jim Fantaci   Cheryl Lachowicz
Christine Duncan and Nelle Nugent
By arrangement with **Andrew Braunsberg**

presents

Richard Dreyfuss Eric Stoltz
Bob Dishy René Auberjonois Bronson Pinchot
Rachel York and Elizabeth Berkley

in

"SLY FOX"

by

Larry Gelbart

with

Professor Irwin Corey   Nick Wyman

**Charles Antalosky   Linda Halaska   Jeremy Hollingworth
Robert LaVelle   Jason Ma   Jeff Talbott   Gordon Joseph Weiss**

and

Peter Scolari

Scenic Design	Costume Design	Lighting Design	Sound Design
George Jenkins **Jesse Poleshuck**	**Albert Wolsky**	**Phil Monat**	**T. Richard Fitzgerald** **Carl Casella**

Wigs By	Casting	Technical Supervision
Paul Huntley	**Stuart Howard & Amy Schecter, CSA**	**Teckeneally, Inc.**

Marketing	Fight Staging	Associate Producers
TMG—The Marketing Group	**B.H. Barry**	**Aaron Levy, Jill Furman** **Debra Black, Peter May**

Production Stage Manager	Press Representative	General Manager
Marybeth Abel	**The Publicity Office**	**Peter Bogyo**

Directed By

Arthur Penn

CAST

(in order of apperance)

SIMON ABLE...Eric Stoltz
SLY'S SERVANTS...........................Jeremy Hollingworth
Charles Antalosky
Linda Halaska
FOXWELL J. SLY..............................Richard Dreyfuss
LAWYER CRAVEN..............................Bronson Pinchot
JETHRO CROUCH..............................Rene Auberjonois
ABNER TRUCKLE...Bob Dishy
MISS FANCY..Rachel York
MRS. TRUCKLE....................................Elizabeth Berkley
CROUCH'S SERVANT....................................Jason Ma
CAPTAIN CROUCH.....................................Nick Wyman
THE CHIEF OF POLICE..............................Peter Scolari
1ST POLICEMAN....................................Robert LaVelle
2ND POLICEMAN/BAILIFE................Gordon Joseph Weiss
3RD POLICEMAN..Jeff Talbott
COURT CLERK................................Professor Irwin Corey
THE JUDGE......................................Richard Dreyfuss

San Francisco
One day in the late 1800's

ACT ONE
SCENE 1. Sly's Bedroom.
SCENE 2. Truckle Living Room.
SCENE 3. Crouch's Office.
SCENE 4. Sly's Bedroom.

ACT TWO
SCENE 1. A Jail Cell.
SCENE 2. The Courtroom.
SCENE 3. Sly's Bedroom.

ACT 1

SCENE 1

(The bedroom of FOXWELL J. SLY. SPACIOUS and well appointed, it is empty just now. There are windows up stage center, shutters closed to block out the morning sun; doors up stage, stage left, stage right, another entrance stage right is up a short flight of stairs. Prominent is a huge canopied bed - SLY'S "sickbed", whose interior can be cut off by curtains. These are open, the bed linens are rumpled. A wheel chair is parked before an armoire up stage right. Street sounds are heard, the church bell wakens with a muffled toll. Then, SLY moans pathetically off stage, behind the up left down stage door. Able appears in down stage left door, speaking back to it.)

ABLE. Yes, Mister Sly, right away, sir! *(Going to the windows.)* Just give me a moment to let in the light. *(He opens the shutters. As he crosses to the bell pull.)* A second or two while I re-set the scene. *(He flicks a good deal of water from a silver pitcher onto the bedding; then, calls out.)* Let's go, everyone! Ho! Up here! He's awake! Sly's awake! Bring fresh sheets and pillow cases!

(As THREE SERVANTS ENTER:)

ABLE. *(Continued.)* Sweeten the air. His bed is awash in sweat. Mister Sly spent another night in agony. I doubt he slept an hour. The poor bugger gets no rest at all. If he's to die in his sleep, God'll have to be on his toes.

(As THE SERVANTS tidy up, change the bed:)

THIRD SERVANT. *(Sympathetically.)* He gets worse and worse.
ABLE. Worse than you can imagine.

SECOND SERVANT. How can he bear it?

ABLE. Here now, you know he can't stand long faces. Always give him your best, fake smiles. The worse he looks, the better you'll pretend. The more you love him, the more you'll lie.

FIRST SERVANT. We do our best, Able.

ABLE. That we do. Now, finish up. I'll fetch the old man off the toilet, after I remind why he went. *(He goes to the Down Stage left door, calls in.)* Mister Sly, sir, good morning sir. *(SLY moans Off Stage.)* Let me help you, sir. *(He EXITS Down Stage left door. SERVANTS finish their work, as we hear, Off Stage:)* Here, sir. Lean on me. Slowly, sir.

(FOXWELL J. SLY, his face etched in pain, enters through Down Stage left door in his nightgown, and cap supported by ABLE. SERVANTS greet him with "Good morning, sir", "God bless you, sir.")

SLY. Thank you, good people, thank you. Decent of you to try to cheer me. Where will I find such good help after I'm dead? Able. *(As ABLE leads him to his wheel chair.)* What a night! My breath searing my lungs with pain, my fever bright enough to read by. *(Contact with the chair seat causes him to moan.)* My legs cramped up double like fire tongs.

ABLE. *(Prompting SERVANTS.)* Our prayers were with you, sir.

THIRD SERVANT. Our prayers were with you, sir.

FIRST SERVANT. All our prayers.

SECOND SERVANT. *(Enthusiastically.)* You look wonderful, sir!

SLY. You are jewels, each of you, my real treasure, my only joy. And now, if you will leave me, it is time for my morning suffering. *(He turns away from them. When THE SERVANTS have exited, to ABLE:)* Are they gone?

ABLE. Gone. I pronounce you cured! I pronounce you well!

SLY. Well? Me? *(He sits up smartly.)* No one's better! No one's more fit! *(Getting out of the chair.)* I've got enough health to start another man! Catch me sick with a new day dawning? The bay shimmering like

SLY FOX

diamonds, the hills as green as cash? The sun the color of gold? Ah, bright, glimmering, warming gold, the centerpiece of the sky! Gold, hiding and teasing under the ground. To find it, to fondle it, the best reason for living. To lie next to it in the earth, the only advantage of dying. *(Crosses up to the window.)* Able. *(As ABLE crosses to join him.)* Look at that parade of fools. *(They look down at the scene below.)* Dumber'n their donkeys. They'll do anything for gold. Pan-handler, miner, thief - they'll beg, burrow or steal it. Each of them lost in a twenty-four carat heat. Night brings no sleep and they dream all through the day, dream of gold, only gold - God with an "l", gold. But I have no need to dream. Mine's come true. I already own what those simps below slobber and kill for. *(He crosses to the heavy chest at the foot of the bed.)* And my back has yet to bend. My hands have yet to know a blister. I've used only the muscle of my mind. For all that I have, I have gained by wit - using my own and what others lack of it. *(He unlocks the chest, throws it open. Then, gazing fondly at the chest's gleaming contents.)* This is where gold belongs. Not in the sky above or the earth below, but here - with me! For the sight of it, the feel of it. Here, where it serves the delightful double purpose of enriching me, while depriving someone else. *(Noticing ABLE's indiffernce.)* Able, do I detect a sudden, unseemly lack of greed?

ABLE. What I feel is pity, sir.

SLY. Pity? No man pities me.

ABLE. Pity for the gold jailed up in there.

SLY. And you? What would you do with it?

ABLE. If I had the power? I'd give it wings. I'd let it glisten in the light.

SLY. Able, Able, you don't free gold. You covet, you coddle, you cuddle it. Fondle a coin long enough, if begins to feel like skin. Are you saying that were I to leave you all this in my will - a document for which I have no need since they're only for people who're going to die - are you saying you'd get rid of it all?

ABLE. Every bit! Fast as I could! For the best of all possible uses!

SLY FOX

For women! Round, naked, pink, black, or yellow. Five fine women. One for each limb! *(Reaches into the chest, scoops up a handful of coins.)* Drinks on Simon Able, all up and down, in every saloon and groggery on the Barbary Coast! The whole town with a hangover, courtesy of me! Silk! Silk! I'd have the worms working overtime. Silk sheets! Silk shirts! Silk hankies! One blow and I'd give 'em to the orphans. Europe! A trip to Paris, France, where I hear they've yet to invent bloomers. London next. On to England to let the Queen meet me. Then, home to a house like this, with my own attic full of servants. Wine-swilling, gin-guzzling, loveable, humble lackies like me.

(He bows "humbly".)

SLY. Ninny! No wonder you've botched your life, buried yourself in debt. *(Touching the chest's top layer of coins.)* You never disturb them. You let them rest quietly, side by side, and watch the show they buy. People crawl out of the woodwork, they squeeze through the plumbing to offer you everything. Women appear in your linen, merchants lose money for a chance to get yours, and men doff their hats even before you come round the corner. They need only smell it - and you mustn't let them have more than one whiff, these leeches - and they fall into your hands, soused on greed. Able, in all of our time together, have you ever seen one coin escape that chest?

ABLE. The traffic is all one way.

(SLY drops the coins back into the chest.)

SLY. And do I live badly? My wine is as thick as my rugs. My silver is sterling. My glass rings crystal. My shirts are boiled in Hawaii and pressed in Canton.

ABLE. No one lives better. You're a prince of luxury and lust.

SLY. Well, father was a stallion, I can't let him down.

ABLE. Your reputation grows nightly.

SLY. How do people speak of me? Be brutally honest, I can take a compliment.

ABLE. Everyone honors you, pays respect, pays tribute, pays courtesy.

SLY. Pays, pays, my favorite verb. And why am I revered? The rich old bugger is ill, they soon learn; hopelessly, mortally ill. Better than that, there's nary a widow in the wings, no soon-to-be orphans praying their little knees raw. Their spittle accrues, their seats grow moist. I need only to pretend to be at death's door, and it's a case of love at first sight.

(A knock is heard Off Stage Right.)

SLY. Ah! The first viper of the day! See who it is whose greed gets up with the sun. *(ABLE looks through peep hole in Stage Right door.)*

ABLE. It's Lawyer Craven.

SLY. Ah, Lawyer Craven - the early bird who is also the worm.

(As ABLE EXITS door Stage Right. SLY has a sip of wine.)

SLY. Dying gives me such an appetite.

ABLE. *(Re-entering.)* I told him to wait. That we were changing your bed - I said you'd soiled it during the night.

SLY. Nice touch.

ABLE. Let me stash these dainties. *(As he hides the breakfast tray in the up Stage nightstand, and places a tray loaded with medication on the one down stage.)* And put out our tinctures and our mixtures.

SLY. *(Grimaces.)* There's enough medicine there to make you sick.

ABLE. Your shawl.

(He drapes a shawl on SLY's shoulders.)

SLY. Time to suffer once more. To sob and sigh, to moan.

ABLE. And groan.

SLY. I know my business. You get 'em ready. You set 'em alongside the stool, I'll milk 'em. *(Getting into bed.)* Let me get into my deathbed and we can open shop. *(ABLE hands him nightcap.)* Show him in. We'll have slaughtered lamb for breakfast!

(He falls back on the pillows, his face a portrait of pain. ABLE closes the bed curtains, so that SLY is hidden from view. He then opens Stage Right door to admit CRAVEN, battered briefcase in hand, dressed in black and all that his name implies.)

ABLE. Lawyer Craven.

CRAVEN. *(Nods.)* Able. *(Looking at the bed.)* How's he doing?

ABLE. The end is in sight.

CRAVEN. Yes, but when? My God, I've seen redwoods go quicker!

ABLE. Soon enough, sir, soon enough. He's just a rattle away from death. *(Lowering his voice.)* Did you - uh - bring the will, so I can have him fill it out?

CRAVEN. *(Producing the document.)* Complete. All it wants is his signature.

ABLE. I'll see to that.

CRAVEN. And here — *(Pointing.)* I've left space to write in the heir he's named. If I wrote it, the world being full of suspicion, some might think I set him onto it myself, but if he designates me as his heir in his own hand, no court will contest it, despite the vicious, filthy things people whisper behind my back.

ABLE. *(Taking the will.)* Right. *(Fishing.)* Is this all you brought? Only the will?

CRAVEN. *(Unhappily producing a gold goblet from his briefcase.)* Solid gold!

ABLE. It's glorious. It belongs in a church.

CRAVEN. I just hope they don't miss it. Show it to him. Say I made a gift of it.

ABLE. How well you know the human heart. It it any wonder, with your experience? *(Drawing the bed curtains open.)* This'll please him. *(Quietly.)* Mister Sly? *(SLY stirs.)* Sir? Lawyer Craven's here to ask after you.

SLY. Dear Craven. The first as always.

ABLE. He's brought a goblet to drink to your health.

SLY. Ah, Craven. In this sad world of sniveling, self-serving brown-noses, he is truly a standout.

ABLE. *(Aside, to Craven.)* Did I lie?

SLY. *(Reaching out pathetically.)* Able? Is the good man here? I see so poorly. The doctors say I mustn't use my eyes and ears at the same time.

CRAVEN. *(Crossing to the bed.)* Precious friend Sly. I've come to wish you health, certainly better that the miserable one you've been enjoying.

SLY. I am grateful, sir. I would've thanked you, had I lived.

CRAVEN. Surely, you still —

SLY. *(Cutting in.)* Living is all that keeps me from dying. My body is a container of pain. Its main ingredient is bile. Its chief industry indigestion. And my kidneys have gone into business for themselves.

ABLE. *(Pressing the goblet into SLY's hand.)* Maybe Mr. Craven's gift'll change your luck, sir.

SLY. *(Holding it close to his "failing" eyes.)* It's gold, am I right? Gold?

CRAVEN. If only I could bring you comfort instead.

SLY. Indeed. What good are my riches now, now that my heart beats only once an hour?

CRAVEN. Oh, how I pray for you.

(He kneels on the chest at the foot of the bed and caresses it, during:)

SLY. It cannot last much longer. May the Lord pardon my sins. I was too attached to money and now it suffocates my soul. I have swindled people!

CRAVEN. You? Never! You are the most honorable man I know in all San Francisco.

SLY. How can I think God enough for letting me know men like you? Craven, Craven! True friend. Good friend. Best friend!

ABLE. *(To CRAVEN, as HE begins closing the bed curtains.)* You hear?

CRAVEN. *(To SLY.)* The closer to death, the closer I feel toward you.

SLY. *(Looking toward the heavens, "deliriously".)* Mother! Mommy!

ABLE. *(Finished closing the curtains, to CRAVEN.)* Any questions?

CRAVEN. *(Joyfully.)* We're almost there!

ABLE. He's almost there. He's just a headstone's throw away from eternity.

CRAVEN. He's not too weak to finish the will? Have you got enough ink? Can I sharpen your quill?

ABLE. Leave it to me.

CRAVEN. I won't forget you when this is over. I'll treat you as good as my own.

ABLE. Perhaps a - uh - a small deposit on your gratitude? *(CRAVEN hands ABLE a small coin.)* You are Christian beyond belief, sir.

(A knock at door Stage Right.)

CRAVEN. *(Worried.)* Who's that?

ABLE. Maybe the doctor. Or the priest. Both just as helpful, the only difference is their fee. Perhaps you should —

(Door Stage Right opens; a SERVANT enters, addresses ABLE.)

THIRD SERVANT. Mister Crouch is here. They're helping him climb the stairs.

(THE SERVANT EXITS.)

SLY FOX

CRAVEN. Crouch! What's that miser up to? He doesn't take one step uphill unless it's for profit.

ABLE. *(Thinking fast.)* He's coming to appraise the jewels, the estate. You'd better go, sir.

CRAVEN. And leave that bloodsucker alone with what's to be mine?

ABLE. Trust me. I'll guard your interests.

(Through door Stage Right, CROUCH ENTERS. An ancient, tottering man, he is supported by a gold handled cane.)

CROUCH. Craven. Ah hah! I thought I smelled lawyer here.

CRAVEN. Well, Jethro Crouch, in the flesh. Or, at least, what's left of it.

CROUCH. I'm still alive. The Lord's been kind to me.

CRAVEN. God is respectful of his elders. Much as I would like to stay and exchange mumbles —*(Crossing to the door.)* The sight of you is always reassuring, sir. You are absolute proof of life after death.

(And he goes.)

CROUCH. What's he want here?

ABLE. He's just hovering, making lazy circles over the bed, waiting to pick the pocket in Sly's shroud,

CROUCH. *(Parting the bed curtain slightly with his cane, HE peeks in and cackles.)* I love to look at dying men. I've seen so many, but you never see the same one twice. In my eighty years I've buried four brothers, my sister, father, mother, friends, enemies, a wife I was deeply devoted to, three mistresses and I'm still alive. I've been pallbearer to men I seen christened. Watched 'em go from pink babies to blue stiffs. And I go on and on. *(Nods at the bed.)* Now, this one. How's he doing?

ABLE. Bad, very bad.

CROUCH. Good as that, huh? Nearing the end, you'd say?

ABLE. Inches away.

CROUCH. How's his pulse?

ABLE. Faint.

CROUCH. Weak?

ABLE. Weak as a whore's promise.

CROUCH. His breath?

ABLE. With enough rasp to file a lock.

CROUCH. *(Gleefully.)* Music, music! What about his tongue?

ABLE.Thick and hard. You could make a wallet out of it.

CROUCH.Then he's almost there! I've seen the routine so often, I could die with my eyes shut. Soon, no air. Pale. Then, they get a little purpiley. Then, clammy. Then, no feeling. Ears dulled, lids yellow. Oh, it's the greatest show on earth!

ABLE. That's him to a tee. He lays there like a log since this morning. He hears nothing, is nothing!

CROUCH. Truly! *(ABLE gestures "Watch", then pulls the bed curtain aside. After an appreciative gasp:)* Beautiful!!

ABLE. *(Loudly, to the "sleeping" SLY.)* Hey, Sly! Not dead yet, you bag of pus in a nightgown? What're you up to, you pinchpenny? Figuring out some way to take it with you?

CROUCH. *(Prodding the bed with his cane.)* Here, stand up, corpse! Face the old man! How's it feel not to feel? Your legs only good for spasms? What's it like, laying in bed with only death to make love to? *(As ABLE closes the bed curtains:)* Mock old Crouch, eh? I'll out-last you all. When you're six feet under, I'll live in your houses and gum all your food! *(As, behind CROUCH'S back, SLY hands CRAVEN's goblet to ABLE:)* Have the will ready! I'll want all the money I lent back, first thing.

ABLE. I think that'll take some time.

CRAVEN. Time? I hate time!

ABLE. Lawyer Craven means to add some new - what do you call 'em - clauses to Sly's will.

CROUCH. New clauses? He's not changing Sly's promise to remember me for all that's flown from my pockets into his? What's that ratbag, Craven, up to?

ABLE. *(Handing CROUCH the goblet.)* He gave him this.

CROUCH. *(Examining goblet.)* There's one just like it in my church.

ABLE. *(Nodding toward the bed.)* The poor fool measures friendship by presents. If I were you, I'd give him even more. You've got to stay in the race.

CROUCH. I can't keep competing. I've got nothing more to give. I'm a poor man.

ABLE. What about that ring?

CROUCH. This ring? Never! Never! My wife was buried with this ring! (He turns, heads for the door Stage Right. ABLE goes to the chest, opens it and puts the goblet in.) No, sir. He's gotten the last he's getting! Too much is more than he can have! *(He turns back to ABLE and sees the shimmering gold in the open chest. Almost bent in half with greed, he beckons to ABLE, as he removes his ring.)* Here, give it to him! If he wakes up before he dies, tell him it was a little going away present. But, mind, I want it back the minute he croaks!

ABLE. With all I have to do, I hope I remember.

CROUCH. *(Slapping a coin into ABLE's hand.)* You'll remember! Just say you've got to return the ring to his nearest and dearest friend. I don't care if you have to cut his finger off to get it!

(CROUCH EXITS door Stage Right. SLY pulls the bed curtains aside.)

SLY. Is he gone?

ABLE. For years.

SLY. You got rid of him just in time. I almost split a gut. *(Getting out of bed and opening the chest.)* Able, of all my pupils, you are the best.

ABLE. There is no greater praise, sir.

SLY. An outstanding swindler. When you're free of your debt to me, there's no telling to what height you will finally stoop. *(Extending*

CRAVEN'S goblet.)

The ring. *(ABLE drops CROUCH's ring into the goblet.)* The bribes. *(ABLE drops CROUCH's and CRAVEN's coins into the goblet.)* I'll put these against your account.

ABLE. *(A wry smile.)* Very generous, sir. At this rate, we'll be even in two hundred years.

SLY. *(At his desk, writing in his ledger.)* Now, now. It wasn't I who misspent your youth, my boy. I'm not the gambler who changed cash into chips, and chips into chits, and handed out enough I.O.U's to paper the Taj Mahal.

ABLE. *(Fondly.)* Well, whatever I lost at the tables, I'm ahead in memories. *(And remember he does.)* Champagne for breakfast. Beautiful nights, some lasting weeks at a time. Finding surprise cash in forgotten pockets. Green felt covered with bets. Lovelies at my elbow. Slender hands at my back. And then, as they will, the cards froze, went cold - so cold every King, Queen and Jack went south, leaving me for company only three's and four's and all the other vagrants in the deck.

SLY. You put your trust in luck. I'm not a great believer in either. You'll learn from me. Better than in that debtor's prison I took you from. And when you've paid back all the money I laid out for you —

ABLE. *(Pouring wine for SLY.)* Plus the nominal usury.

SLY. From then on, you'll play people, not poker. You'll learn there's more to be gained from their greed than a thirteen-card royal flush, with a cherry on top.

ABLE. Now, this is the way I like to see you.

SLY. Ah, Able. You drink with me. You rob, cheat, and whore with me. You are the son I never had. *(Raising his glass.)* To my oh, so devoted friends. I'll be at both your graves - watching the worms tuck in for a picnic. *(A sip of wine, then.)* I've been too kind to them, Able. I have been much too kind!

(The doorbell rings Off Stage.)

SLY FOX

SLY. Ah hah! What thief is that?

ABLE. *(Crosses to the window, looks down.)* It's Abner Truckle.

SLY. Ah, dear, dear Truckle. At last a man whose sincerity is apparent. It's written on both his faces.

ABLE. *(Crossing to bed.)* Back on your back. Crank up the wheezes.

SLY. When's the last time I threw a fit?

ABLE. Saturday.

SLY. Too soon for another. Fetch him.

(He gets into bed and closes the curtains. ABLE, at door Stage Right, admits the joyless TRUCKLE.)

ABLE. Good morning, Mr. Truckle.

TRUCKLE. *(Getting right down to business.)* Is he dead?

ABLE. He's napping.

TRUCKLE. Napping again? All he does is nap. What would he miss if he was dead?

ABLE. You can afford patience, sir. You know he means to leave you everything.

TRUCKLE. He does? You're sure?

ABLE. That's all I work for.

TRUCKLE. How close is he?

ABLE. He prays to God to let him die.

TRUCKLE. I've brought a little something to add power to his prayer. *(Producing a small bottle.)* Just one drop of this in a glass of wine and he'll never sleep more deeply.

(He pours some into SLY's wine glass.)

ABLE. That smells of foul play.

TRUCKLE. It smells of nothing, that's what's so good about it. You can tell him it's for his rest, you won't be lying.

ABLE. He'll never take it. He has no faith in medicines. I keep trying to get him a good doctor.

TRUCKLE. For God's sake, no doctors! Sometimes they actually help. If a man's going to die, let him die. This long, drawn-out torture. The pain. The agony. How much can I take?

ABLE. I know it's been hell for you, sir.

TRUCKLE. *(A new tack.)* I have a friend! *(Crosses to windows, points Off Stage.)* He works across the road at the ship chandlers. He can put a harpoon through a whale from two hundred feet. Tomorrow morning, get Sly to the window for a breath of air and bam! *(Smacks his forehead.)* Right through his blow-hole!

ABLE. Sir, control yourself.

TRUCKLE. Why should I?

ABLE. You don't want him dead yet.

TRUCKLE. I do! I've waited long enough! He's been sick for months and he's still not dead! I don't think he's trying.

ABLE. But you don't want him to die while his will's still incomplete.

TRUCKLE. Incom-what?

ABLE. Well, it's written, sir, but neither signed nor sealed; and the heir is yet to be named.

TRUCKLE. What!? I was assured the will was complete! You assured me! He assured me! Then you assured his assuring me! Somehow, I felt assured.

ABLE. Yes, yes, but Lawyer Craven —

TRUCKLE. *(Cuts in.)* Craven, the lawyer?

ABLE. He hardly knows Sly and suddenly he's hanging around, giving him free legal advice.

TRUCKLE. *(Loudly.)* Damn!

ABLE. Shh!

TRUCKLE. *(Quietly.)* Damn! Damn these money grubbers! They make my own sincerity seem suspicious.

(He forgetfully raises the poisoned wine to his lips. ABLE grabs the

SLY FOX

goblet from him, goes to the window and pours the contents out. A beat, then a CRY of pain is heard from someone down on the street.)

ABLE. *(Calls down.)* Sorry!

TRUCKLE. *(Shaken, he sits on the chest, and ponders a moment. Then.)* Able!

TRUCKLE. Tell Sly I've made him a partner in my business. *(Handing ABLE a small pouch.)* Say this gold dust is only a start.

ABLE. This news might just make him well.

TRUCKLE. Bite your tongue! Go ahead, tell him.

ABLE. *(Opening the bed curtains.)* Mister Sly. Sir? Your friend —

TRUCKLE. *(Correcting him.)* Best friend.

ABLE. Your best friend, Mister Truckle, has brought you this medicine, sir. *(SLY does not stir. ABLE puts the pouch in SLY's limp hand.)* Gold dust, sir. Not too hard to swallow, eh?

TRUCKLE. *(Stepping forward.)* I'd gladly go before you, friend Sly. My wife lights candles for you all day long. This gold is just a beginning. You'll live to see more. Much more.

SLY. *(Reaching out feebly, with unseeing eyes) Able.(Inches from TRUCKLE's face.)* Send for Abner Truckle. I want to see him.

TRUCKLE. Truckle is here. Look how here he is.

SLY. *(Squinting.)* Ah, Truckle, forgive me. I'm half-way to the other side. It's hard to make out living people.

TRUCKLE. *(Regarding the gold.)* You do realize I've brought you this?

(He tries to lift the pouch from SLY's hand but SLY holds on with a death-like grip.)

SLY. Such goodness. *(Coughs.)* Such kindness. *(Coughs.)* Your friendship fills me with phlegm. *(Coughs.)* Able, my handkerchief!

TRUCKLE. *(Handing him his own.)* Take mine. Please. Everything I have is yours. Keep it.

SLY FOX

(SLY coughs into it, starts to return it.)

SLY. Thank you.

TRUCKLE. No, keep it! Please!

SLY. I'll not forget this, Truckle. You'll see how I remembered you at the end. If only it would come —

(He lies back, exhales an almost death-like rattle. TRUCKLE pulls ABLE aside.)

TRUCKLE. Able, he's got to sign the will! He can't last the day! Fetch a notary!

ABLE. I can't leave him!

TRUCKLE. Go! He's toyed with me long enough! What's mine's been his; now, what's everyone's'll be mine!

ABLE. *(Thinking fast.)* And may you and your most generous wife use it well, sir.

TRUCKLE. *(Troubled.)* Generous?? Most generous? My wife?

ABLE. *(Innocently.)* Mrs. Truckle, sir, the apple of many an eye.

TRUCKLE. I'll not have her name on your tongue! I'll not have my wife on anyone's tongue!

ABLE. But Mrs. Truckle's the toast of the coast, sir. Market Street's never fuller than when she sashays down to church.

TRUCKLE. Sashays!

ABLE. They say the only sight nicer'n seeing her approach is watching her going away.

(TRUCKLE, too incensed to speak, tries to strike ABLE, who dodges.)

TRUCKLE. When she goes to church, you say?

ABLE. Every morning, sir.

TRUCKLE. Who asked you?!

ABLE. You did.

SLY FOX

TRUCKLE. Well, shut up when you answer! *(Crazed, as he EXITS through down stage left door.)* How dare she go to church in front of everyone! Has the woman no sense of shame?!

ABLE. *(Following TRUCKLE.)* Wrong way, sir! *(Dashing through same door.)* You're in the toilet!

TRUCKLE. *(Re-entering with ABLE at his side.)* You think I don't know that's a toilet? *(Hurrying toward down stage right door.)* You think I don't know everything that's going on without my knowing it?! *(And he is out the door.)*

(TRUCKLE gone, SLY sits up in bed.)

SLY. Well done, Able!

ABLE. I had to throw cold water over him. The will was making him come into heat.

SLY. I had no idea the man was so jealous.

ABLE. Insanely so.

SLY. With cause?

ABLE. Mrs. Truckle is very tasty, sir.

SLY. Oh? Start at the top.

ABLE. Her face is serene. If she prayed to be pretty, it worked. Breasts - her breasts could be larger, but then that's always true. She's got a lovely broad beam. A real church pew spread.

SLY. Able, I must see her. If the dish is as tasty as you've described, it should be set before the king.

(The front doorbell rings. ABLE goes to the window.)

ABLE. *(To SLY.)* It's Miss Fancy.

SLY. *(Annoyed.)*. I have no time for whores!

ABLE. Now, that's very unkind. She sleeps with you for nothing and you're not even from City Hall.

SLY. I don't want her around. She could blow the whole gaffe. How long do you think our pigeons would believe I was dying if they knew she was sharing my deathbed?

(He starts for the door Up Stage Right.)

ABLE. Where are you going?

SLY. I'm going down the road to see Mrs. Truckle.

ABLE. But you're supposed to be dying!

SLY. I'll disguise myself - as someone healthy.

ABLE. It's very dangerous.

SLY. Ah, but that's the best reason of all. You get rid of Miss Fancy. Finally, totally rid!

ABLE. And how do I do that?

SLY. Think the way I do: be brilliant! *(He EXITS.)*

MISS FANCY'S VOICE. *(Off Stage.)* That's all right, I know the way!

(Hearing her voice, ABLE dashes to the bed, starts to pull the curtains. He stops as MISS FANCY enters door Down Stage Right.)

MISS FANCY. *(Happily.)* Able, Sly's out of bed!

ABLE. From the look of his absence I'd say that's true, yes.

MISS FANCY. *(Heading for Down Stage Left door.)* Up after all these weeks!

ABLE. *(Running, blocking the door.)* Wait, Miss Fancy! He's - uh - he's not decent!

MISS FANCY. *(Smiles.)* Well, I wouldn't know him if I saw him that way.

(Again, she starts for the door. ABLE leads her away.)

ABLE. You don't want to go in there. He's being covered with leeches. They're bleeding him.

MISS FANCY. The doctor's here?
ABLE. Two.
MISS FANCY. Two doctors!
ABLE. One for his veins, one for his arteries.
MISS FANCY. Dear God!

(He crosses, yanks the bell pull.)

ABLE. One moment! *(He EXITS Down Stage Left door, leaving the distressed MISS FANCY. Urgently, Off Stage:)* Yes, Doctor! Right away, sir! Oh, God, he looks awful!

(He re-enters with a porcelain pan into which he drops some nasty-looking surgical instruments.)

MISS FANCY. Able — *(ABLE yanks the bell pull again, MISS FANCY trailing behind.)* It's all so strange; so very strange.

(SECOND SERVANT ENTERS door Up Stage Left.)

SECOND SERVANT. Able?
ABLE. Bring an empty whiskey bottle. Half a pint'll do. And have Becky bring the spray. No, I'll take care of that.
SECOND SERVANT. Right!

(He EXITS door Up Stage Left, as ABLE crosses to door Up Stage Right.)

ABLE. *(Calling out the door.)* Becky!
MISS FANCY. For weeks Sly and I were close. Every night. Afternoons. I never knew a man could be so close, so often. Last month I take a steamer up the Yukon for a Deacon's convention; I get back'n all I see of him but is his tonics'n tablets. Just exactly what is it that ail's him so bad?

ABLE. His heart is clogged. His blood is clotted. He's got every affliction in the book. For him, death will be a convalescence.

(THIRD SERVANT appears with spray through up Stage Right door.)

THIRD SERVANT. Able!
ABLE. *(Taking spray from her.)* Thank you, luv. Please bring up a brandy for the doctor. Make it a double.
THIRD SERVANT. Right away!

(As the THIRD SERVANT EXITS Stage Left door, ABLE starts spraying in MISS FANCY's direction.)

ABLE. Go, Miss Fancy. Why be part of all this sad and ugly? I'll tell him you came by. It'll cheer him up.
MISS FANCY. I don't want his cheer. *(A pause.)* I want his name.

(She produces a document from her handbag.)

ABLE. What's that?
MISS FANCY. An application for a marriage license. Which he promised to sign — *(Sitting on SLY's bed; patting the mattress.)* Right here, 'fore he came down so godawful ill.
ABLE. Now, why would you want to marry? You're sitting pretty. Your business is booming, your bed needs a traffic cop.
MISS FANCY. And the child I'm 'spectin's goin' to need to have a name.
ABLE. Really? Who's the father, do you know?
MISS FANCY. Well, I'm tryin' to narrow it down - but it's been such a bumper year. Able, won't you help get Sly to sign this 'fore he cashes in? It would do me proud to have the first member of my family born legitimate.

SLY FOX

(SECOND SERVANT ENTERS door Stage Left with an empty whiskey bottle.)

SECOND SERVANT. Able!

(ABLE crosses to him, takes the bottle.)

ABLE. Thanks, lad. *(Handing SECOND SERVANT the spray.)* Spray 'round the bed. Let me get this in there.

(HE EXITS through Down Stage Left door, leaving MISS FANCY alone with the SECOND SERVANT.)

SECOND SERVANT. *(Greeting her fondly.)* How do, Miss Fancy.
MISS FANCY. *(Ever the business woman.)* Long time no see, Charlie.

(ABLE re-enters, speaking over his shoulder into Down Stage Left door.)

ABLE. Yes, doctor. There'll be no more talking out here. Yes, sir. *(To SECOND SERVANT.)* Go! *(SECOND SERVANT EXITS Stage Left door. ABLE crosses to MISS FANCY, starts leading her toward Stage Right door.)* Look, darlin' I appreciate your pickle, but Sly's a lost cause. Why not find someone else? There's plenty of others'd more'n pleased to play daddy for you.
MISS FANCY. Name one.
ABLE. What about old man Crouch? Widowed for ages. Moneyed for even more.
MISS FANCY. Jethro Crouch? *(Frowns.)* Why do I think he's dead?
ABLE. It happens from being in his company. *(Opening Down Stage Right door.)* I wouldn't waste any time, though. He's getting bids from the undertakers himself.
MISS FANCY. *(Stepping to him.)* I'm most grateful, Able. Stop by my place later and I'll show you my thanks.

ABLE. *(An arm around her waist.)* Shall we say about nine o'clock?
MISS FANCY. Make it nine-fifteen. I'm thankin' the Mayor at nine.

(She EXITS door Down Stage Right, just as THIRD SERVANT ENTERS door Up Stage Left with brandy on a tray.)

ABLE. *(Taking the tray.)* Here, my dear. I'll take care of it!

(He starts for Down Stage Left door as she EXITS. ABLE then downs the brandy, without lifting the glass from the tray. SLY suddenly enters Up Stage Right door, wearing a beat-up straw hat and an oriental coat. ABLE is startled.)

SLY. *(Removing the hat.)* I have seen her! *(He tosses the hat to ABLE. Unfastening the coat, handing it to him:)* I borrowed these from Chang. I went to her house, posed as a beggar and there she was!
ABLE. Mrs. Truckle?
SLY. The very same.
ABLE. And?
SLY. And a beggar in fact she has made of me.
ABLE. *(Helping SLY into his robe.)* You're smitten.
SLY. Smote! Able, I must have her!
ABLE. Have Truckle's wife? His jealousy is legendary. He sends her to the country for a week before the iceman comes.
SLY. I mean to have her.
ABLE. You'd have more luck seducing a statue. There is no way it can be done.
SLY. *(Temptingly.)* We spoke earlier, I believe, of reducing your debt.
ABLE. *(Ears up.)* We did.
SLY. When I'm happy, son, I like everyone to be happy.
ABLE. Just how happy were you thinking of making me?
SLY. I thought, if you could arrange a meeting, I'd return, say one hundred dollars worth of your I.O.U.'s.

ABLE. One hundred? You've panted twice that many times since you've seen her. I was thinking of saying no even to two.

SLY. No to two hundred?

ABLE. Clearly you can't gauge Truckle's sickness. He's done all but put birdseed in her bustle so she leaves a trail wherever she goes.

SLY. Would you think of saying to no three?

ABLE. I was thinking more of saying yes to five.

SLY. Five?!

ABLE. Five!

SLY. Done!

ABLE. Truly? Five hundred off?!

SLY. Five hundred! *(He whips open a desk drawer, collects a number of I.O.U.'s, which he slams into the delighted ABLE's hand.)* I am a connoisseur of the flesh, my boy, and pound for pound, tit for tat, I tell you she's worth it. Now - how're you going to do it?

ABLE. How?

SLY. How.

ABLE. How do I get Mrs. Truckle into your bed?

SLY. Yes!

ABLE. How do I get her into your bed without her husband knowing it?

SLY. No!

ABLE. No what, no?

SLY. You are missing the point entirely. Did I say one word about him not knowing about it?

ABLE. You mean you want him to know? Want him to know that-?

SLY. *(Cuts in.)* Bullseye!

(SLY's smile is one of devilish delight.)

ABLE. Sir, be reasonable. I know that Truckle so hungers for your gold, he'd sell his mother for live bait - but if you think he'll stand by while you bounce his wife —

SLY. I don't expect him to stand by. I expect him to deliver her to me. Right here. Walk right through that door, and hand her over.

(A beat, then ABLE puts the I.O.U.'s back into SLY's hand.)

ABLE. No man could be that low.

SLY. My boy, you could drill into Abner Truckle for a year and never strike decent. If you can convince him that he's out of my will unless I have his wife, he'll serve me and the good lady our breakfast in bed. You'll see.

ABLE. How do I even suggest it?

SLY. My money's on you. *(Holding up the I.O.U.'s.)* Better still, your money's on you.

ABLE. *(Bracing himself.)* I'll give it a whack.

SLY. Wait. Cuckholding's fine for Truckle. What about those other two worms?

ABLE. Take pity, sir. There's no more to be had from Craven, not a cent.

SLY. You're sure?

ABLE. The only thing you don't own are his fillings.

SLY. Old Crouch, then.

ABLE. Crouch?

SLY. Something to make that living corpse gasp so hard he sucks himself right out of sight!

ABLE. I can't imagine him parting with another buck.

SLY. *(An inspiration.)* Then have him give away someone else's! His son's!

ABLE. Cheat his own son? He'll never do it!

SLY. He will! He's as low as Truckle. Trust me, Able. There is no corner of the human heart I have not lifted and seen the rot below. On your way now. You've got your morning's work cut out for you.

ABLE. Right. All I have to do is get one man to betray his son and the other to pimp for his wife.

SLY FOX

SLY. You're going to learn the underbelly of human nature today, my boy. Never think too little of people. There's always a little less to be thought.

BLACKOUT

SCENE 2

(THE TRUCKLE living room. A door stage right leads to the front hall, a curtained archway stage left to another part of the house. The angelic MRS. TRUCKLE works at her emberoidery frame. She is surprised by the entrance of her husband, truckle, who has worked himself into a man possessed.)

TRUCKLE. Aha! Caught you didn't I?! Caught you doing your - needlework!

MRS. TRUCKLE. Dear God, Abner. Not the same old jealous fit.

TRUCKLE. No, this is a new jealous fit! I warn you, Simplicity, I can hear a cheating heart beating from a mile away. *(Going to Archway.)* Are you alone?

MRS. TRUCKLE. Alone as always.

TRUCKLE. Alone, alone?

MRS. TRUCKLE. Abner, will you never learn to trust me?

TRUCKLE. Trust? My father trusted my mother - until the day she came home from the baker with poppy seeds all over her back!

MRS. TRUCKLE. But you didn't marry your mother.

TRUCKLE. Who am I to take another man's wife? When did you

last see Simon Able?

MRS. TRUCKLE. I know no Simon Able.

TRUCKLE. Then how'd you know his name?

MRS. TRUCKLE. You just said it.

TRUCKLE. Quick thinking, my dear. The truth, woman! Where have you been since I left this house this morning?

MRS. TRUCKLE. As God is my witness, I have been here the whole time. Here, by the window.

TRUCKLE. *(Angered anew.)* By the open window! Why is it open?

MRS. TRUCKLE. It was so stuffy. A little air.

TRUCKLE. Air? *(Slamming the window shut.)* I've forbidden you a thousand times to hang out the window! Displaying yourself like a cupcake in a sweet shop! Tempting and teasing the base instincts of men who would like nothing better than a chance to do what I don't dare admit to myself I would ask you to do for fear that you might say, "Why not? Let's try it once?"

MRS. TRUCKLE. But you know that I gave up all interest in men the moment I married you.

TRUCKLE. Oh, I'd like to know one day without shame. Know that I had finally bought and paid for the respect of even those I have no use for.

(A knock at Stage Right door. Neither TRUCKLE moves.)

MRS. TRUCKLE. *(Timidly.)* Shall I open?

TRUCKLE. Can't wait to show yourself!

ABLE'S VOICE. *(Outside the door.)* Mr. Truckle!

TRUCKLE. *(To MRS. TRUCKLE.)* Into your room! And don't open your window!

(MRS. TRUCKLE EXITS through the archway curtain. TRUCKLE opens the door to admit ABLE.)

SLY FOX

ABLE. News!

TRUCKLE. He's dead?!

ABLE. Worse.

TRUCKLE. What's worse than dead?

ABLE. He's better.

TRUCKLE. No!

ABLE. It's true.

TRUCKLE. How's that possible?

ABLE. He's had a sudden attack of health.

TRUCKLE. When I saw him he looked awful. My prayers seemed answered. He was ready to die.

ABLE. Well, now he's up on his feet, his cheeks filled with color. The man's come back from the grave.

TRUCKLE. There is no God!

ABLE. It's all the cook's fault. He brought his friend to the house, a railroad coolie. The man opens a bag of needles. He pokes one is Sly's bum, another in his earlobe. Next thing you know, Sly pops out of bed, takes a few steps, does a high kick, and says he's got to have a woman!

TRUCKLE. A woman?!

ABLE. A woman!

TRUCKLE. He was dying!

ABLE. Now, he's up. In every direction. The Chinaman took me aside and said it was dangerous.

TRUCKLE. I would think!

ABLE. Said Sly wasn't strong enough for sexual exertion. It could prove fatal. At the height of ecstasy, he might find himself coming and going at the same time.

TRUCKLE. But if sex harms him, why not? I've known a few old men to die in midstream. By all means, get him a woman!

ABLE. Do I dare?

TRUCKLE. Get him two! We can bury him in an hour with a smile on his face!

ABLE. True, but cheapskate that he is, he wants one for nothing.

TRUCKLE. A woman for nothing? In this town? He'll live forever.

ABLE. Oh, you don't know how greedy some people can be. The minute Lawyer Craven —

TRUCKLE. *(Cuts in anxiously.)* Craven, the lawyer?

ABLE— heard of it, he comes running over to say he's giving his daughter.

TRUCKLE. To Sly? His own daughter?

ABLE. Sixteen years old, and one of the seven sure virgins of 'Frisco. He said he'd bring her 'round, all bathed and preened. Her own father. That's why I've come to warn you. You know the Almighty put an argument between a woman's thighs that no man minds losing. I'm afraid you can kiss your inheritance goodbye.

TRUCKLE. No!

ABLE. *(Starts to leave.)* I'd best get back.

TRUCKLE. *(Panicked.)* No! Wait! Wait! For the love of heaven, wait! I can't let this happen! His own daughter. Disgusting. *(Pause.)* I don't have a daughter!

ABLE. No, sir. You've yet to have a child with the exquisite Mrs. Truckle.

(He starts to go again.)

TRUCKLE. Wait! *(Looking toward the Archway.)* My wife...

ABLE. Your wife?

TRUCKLE. Didn't you say she's beautiful? That she's desirable?

ABLE. There's no one that's more than she of either, no, sir.

TRUCKLE. Able, you know I hold Sly closest to my heart. Certainly more than Craven, that rotten jury rigger.

ABLE. No question in my mind, no sir.

TRUCKLE. Wouldn't it be my duty then, really?

ABLE. Sir?

TRUCKLE. To help him recover, to regain his strength?

ABLE. I would answer in a minute, if I understood.

TRUCKLE. Surely, I can do as well by Sly as any common opportunist.

ABLE. I would certainly hope so, yes, sir.

TRUCKLE. Go! Tell Sly that out of reverence for our friendship, I'll bring Mrs. Truckle to him.

ABLE. You'll do that? Your very own wife?

TRUCKLE. My very own wife. Who - you might remind him - is quite often mistaken for my daughter.

ABLE. You'll deliver her yourself?

TRUCKLE. I can do no less.

ABLE. No, sir, I don't believe you can. My congratulations. You are the craftiest of them all. You'll secure a lifetime of riches providing Sly with just a few moments of joy.

TRUCKLE. If he lasts that long.

(They laugh.)

ABLE. True. In his present condition, if he's given the right stroke, he just might have one.

(They laugh again. TRUCKLE's laugh turns into a whimper, then:)

TRUCKLE. Run! Tell him I'll be there in an hour!
ABLE. *(Prompting.)* With?
TRUCKLE. Mrs. Truckle!
ABLE. Clever devil!

(He EXITS door Stage Right, TRUCKLE still laughing. As soon as the door is closed TRUCKLE stops laughing, realizes the enormity of what he's about to to do. He looks toward archway. Then, ducking down, so as not to observed by the religious objects atop the mantle, HE goes to the Archway, and brings MRS. TRUCKLE onstage.)

TRUCKLE. Ah, my dear, you're crying. If I've been hurtful, it's only out of love. *(Kneeling.)* My heart and I are on our knees. Forgive me.

MRS. TRUCKLE. How sweet to have you gentle once more. So often I have prayed to the good Virgin to cure you of your groundless jealousy.

TRUCKLE. She and I have heard your prayers. And we've both worked a way to prove my trust in you.

MRS. TRUCKLE. I can open a window?

TRUCKLE. No, no, no, far more. You and I are going calling on Foxwell Sly. *(Taking her hand.)* To show how true I know you to be, I'll leave you at his side to nurse him, to minister to him with these dainty little fingers that go all the way down to the tips of your saintly little hands.

MRS. TRUCKLE. He means this much to you?

TRUCKLE. His life is very valuable to me. I can't even guess how much.

MRS. TRUCKLE. This is a great honor you pay me, husband.

TRUCKLE. I'll get mine. Let's go!

MRS. TRUCKLE. *(Heading for the mantle.)* First, I must pray.

TRUCKLE. *(Impatiently.)* Now??

MRS. TRUCKLE. I must pray to the Virgin.

TRUCKLE. Give her the morning off! Come!

MRS. TRUCKLE. *(Starting for the Archway.)* I'll need my Bible.

TRUCKLE. *(Stopping her.)* He's got a Bible. I looked at it; it's just like yours. "In the beginning God created" - right?

BLACKOUT

SCENE 3

(CROUCH's office. A rat's nest; sparsely furnished. CROUCH, his jeweler's loupe hanging round his neck addresses his ASIAN SERVANT.)

CROUCH. To see me? A woman? You're sure?

ASIAN SERVANT. Yes, Mr. Crouch.

CROUCH. Who could it be?

ASIAN SERVANT. She didn't say.

CROUCH. *(Thinking aloud.)* A young woman for me — *(Pauses; to himself.)* The little flower girl! Maybe she's pregnant! No, couldn't be - that was twenty years ago. *(To SERVANT.)* Probably come to borrow. Show her in.

(THE SERVANT shows MISS FANCY in, bows, and EXITS.)

MISS FANCY. It's swell of you to give me your valuable time, Mister Crouch.

CROUCH. Time's not as valuable as money. There's many's got more years than dollars.

MISS FANCY. How wise you are.

CROUCH. I knew that before you came. State your business.

MISS FANCY. Mind if I sit, sir?

CROUCH. Sit, sit, sit.

(He nods at the mess of a divan. About to sit, MISS FANCY notices something behind it, screams loudly.)

MISS FANCY. Is that a dead cat?

CROUCH. You know what it costs to feed 'em? Sit, sit!

MISS FANCY. *(Sitting.)* Oh, I'm so tired. So tired of this earthly world. What's it all worth, my bein' rich as Croesus, and as beautiful as everyone says I am? But what's a lady's heaving heart got to do with you, you're probably won'drin'?

CROUCH. I ain't wonderin' nuthin'.

MISS FANCY. Where you come in is, I've got this sudden, spiritual case of the hots to join a nunnery, and I thought if I could sell my jewelry and give the cash to the good sisters, I might be makin' a down payment on a little nook in Paradise. I was told you'd give me an honest appraisal; that you was a very upright gent.

CROUCH. Some people'll say anything. Show me what's for sale.

MISS FANCY. Well, this ring for one. *(CROUCH takes her hand, examines the ring.)* How cold your hand is.

CROUCH. What do I need a warm hand for?

MISS FANCY. You should have a fur coat.

CROUCH. Can't afford one.

MISS FANCY. I'll send you one of mine. It's easy to see no one takes care of you.

CROUCH. My wife died forty years ago.

MISS FANCY. And you never remarried?

CROUCH. Never found anyone to fit her clothes. *(Sits beside her, examines her ring.)* Fine stone. Genuine. Clean fire. This is quality. Yes.

MISS FANCY. It's only one of the little one's daddy left me.

CROUCH. He knew his stuff. Worth two thousand, I'd say.

MISS FANCY. Mercy! So much for so little?

(She places a hand on his knee and works it with her fingers. They are two professionals at work.)

CROUCH. Quality's quality. Two thousand easy. *(Without looking down.)* I can feel that, you know.

MISS FANCY. My hand?

CROUCH. *(Still not looking.)* Whatever's down there. *(Returns the ring.)* What else you got to sell?

MISS FANCY. How 'bout this?

(She spreads her bodice a bit, baring a good deal of bosom and coming even closer to him.)

CROUCH. *(Squinting at chain.)* Gold...heavy gold...

MISS FANCY. The medallion's the real prize. *(Addressing the medallion.)* Let's go, little bird. *(Purrs to Crouch.)* Doesn't want to leave its warm nest.

(She pulls the medallion slowly, tantalizing from between her breasts.)

CROUCH. Mmmm.

MISS FANCY. *(Edging closer.)* Take a good look.

CROUCH. *(He does.)* You've got some nice things.

MISS FANCY. Thank you. And what about the jewelry?

(CROUCH takes a square of green felt from his vest pocket and lays it on her bare chest, using it as a work surface. He looks at the medallion through his loupe.)

CROUCH. Worth five thousand, I'd say.I'd give you three for it right now.

MISS FANCY. That's most generous of you, sir.

CROUCH. *(Putting away the felt.)* I suppose that can happen.

MISS FANCY. *(Offering the medallion.)* Would you like to put it back? *(Placing it in CROUCH's hand.)* Put it back again, the poor little orphan, between the two nuns. *(Her hand guiding his, CROUCH puts the medallion between her breasts. SHE traps his hand in her dress top and holds it there, as she goes on.)* I'd like to show you everything I've got. So you can help me sell it all. I mean, what good is so much trash when a body — *(Moving his hand so that's really trapped in her bosom:)* — has no one close to share it with? No one near, no one dear? Oh, there's lots of fuzz-cheeked boys, no-hipped peacocks, just dying to get

into my wealth. Findin' men's never been my problem. I attract 'em like flies. What I'm talkin' 'bout is someone with real deepness. Wherever do I find such a one? Where does a lady uncover a serious, reliable man she can put her faith in? Someone she can really look up at? Someone like you, sir. *(Pause, then.)* Sir? *(CROUCH emits a short snore.)* Sir?!
ASIAN SERVANT. *(Entering.)* Sir!

(THE SERVANT's voice awakens CROUCH.)

CROUCH. *(Looks at THE SERVANT; then, in puzzlement at his hand inside the top of Miss Fancy's dress.)* Did I just ring for him?
MISS FANCY. *(Disgusted.)* You fell asleep.
CROUCH. *(Removes his hand.)* Damn it! Happens every time I get excited.
ASIAN SERVANT. Mister Crouch, you got a visitor. Mister Able.
CROUCH. Able here? Let him in, quick! *(To MISS FANCY.)* You have to go! I got business.
MISS FANCY. *(Sarcastically.)* Well, I certainly do thank you for your valuable time, sir.

(She crosses to the door as ABLE ENTERS.)

ABLE. *(Bowing deeply.)* Ah, madame, I'm doubled in half by this honor. *(Sotto.)* How'd you do with him?
MISS FANCY. I'd've had more luck with his cane.

(She EXITS.)

CROUCH. Able! What brings you?
ABLE. My concern for you. Sly's purplin' by the minute.
CROUCH. *(High pitched.)* Yay!
ABLE. In two hours, the notary's coming, The doctor's prepared a powder to give Sly just enough strength to hold a pen. Everything's ready,

the whole shootin' match's at stake - now!

CROUCH. Did you show him my ring?

ABLE. The minute Truckle saw it, he gave him a better one. And Craven came running in with an envelope swollen with cash. They're closing in for the finish. They'll be stuffing presents into his coffin.

CROUCH. I can't give any more. *(Rubbing his cane's gold handle fitfully.)* I'm a poor man.

ABLE. Help is my middle name.

CROUCH. Yes? How?

ABLE. If you could give me just one thing - one certain thing - it would put you first in Sly's heart. And that particular thing'll cost you absolutely nothing.

CROUCH. I can afford that!

ABLE. Except for a pittance for the notary so he waits till I bring it to him.

CROUCH. Bring it what to him, bring him?

ABLE. A simple sheet of paper.

CROUCH. I got paper.

ABLE. You just make out a will —

CROUCH. I've got a will, too!

ABLE. In this one, you name Sly your sole heir.

CROUCH. Sly my sole — ?

ABLE. *(Talking fast.)* Heir, sole, him, right! I'll take it to him, prop his eyelids open and show him what a real friend is! How you've left him everything, everything you own!

CROUCH. Instead of my son?

ABLE. What can Sly do then but name you his sole heir?

CROUCH. *(Doubtfully.)* Disinheriting my own son —

ABLE. For only a few hours. Sly won't last the night.

CROUCH. He won't?

ABLE. He's three feet under already. The minute he kicks off, you'll have made your son twice again as rich!

CROUCH. I won't have to keep my word!

SLY FOX

ABLE. What could be nicer? Run!

CROUCH. *(Happily.)* Right! I can still run. *(Crosses to the door, stops.)* Things just don't go by as fast.

(He EXITS.)

ABLE. *(Closes the door, calls after CROUCH mockingly.)* Keep moving, you cadaver - before some dog buries you for bones! *(Shakes his head.)* By God, Sly was right. There is no bottom to greed. A son's as easily bartered as a wife. To think I even talked of pity. This bunch! They'd sell Christ's cross for lumber if they could, or a whisker from God's beard.

(Enter CROUCH'S son, THE CAPTAIN; big, brusque, exaggeratedly military.)

THE CAPTAIN. What're you doing in my father's house, scum?

ABLE. Scum? We've never met, sir. Only those who know me call me scum.

THE CAPTAIN. I know you. You're Foxwell Sly's lackey. His footstool. His nose rag.

ABLE. You've certainly got a gift for coarseness. Truth to tell, my calling's no less respectable than yours.

THE CAPTAIN. You, an indentured slave, dare compare yourself to an officer of the United States Navy, with decorations too numerous not to mention? It's fathoms beneath me even to talk to a man who owns neither his life nor his very soul.

ABLE. Ah, but you mistake my station, sir. I am one of those picked out by the Almighty Himself to see that the world doesn't get boring. And to keep money from becoming moldy, to help the wealth flow from the stupid to the clever, into the streets from out of the floorboards, from under each mattress. If we didn't poke it awake now and then, we good-for-nothings, the world'd go to sleep. To each his own task. I leave it to you to fight the wars and fumble the peace. There's still the rich to rook and the sheep to be shorn, And that's my job, dear Captain, but to do it you must have a brain in your head, not just a brass tourniquet around it and an anchor tattooed on each ball.

(He starts to go.)

THE CAPTAIN. *(Grabbing ABLE's vest roughly.)* How wasted my heroism is in defense of dogs like you!

ABLE. *(Trying to release himself.)* Steady now, Admiral!

THE CAPTAIN. *(Dumping ABLE on divan.)* Worm! Is your vanity so pumped up by favor seekers, you've forgotten how to show respect for second generation wealth?

ABLE. *(Snaps.)* Too bad you'll never see a penny of it!

THE CAPTAIN. And what is that meant to convey?

ABLE. I'm afraid you'd be miserable if you knew. *(Pause, then.)* Which is probably the best reason for telling you. As everyone knows, your old man's filthy rich.

THE CAPTAIN. For a fact.

ABLE. He doesn't spend a wrong buck.

THE CAPTAIN. Right.

ABLE. It's no secret that one pair of underwear has served him a lifetime.

THE CAPTAIN. So?

ABLE. Naturally, you reckon you'll get it all when he dies, but I know better.

THE CAPTAIN. What?

ABLE. At this moment, he's preparing to cut you out of his will, to make someone else his only heir.

THE CAPTAIN. You're lying!

ABLE. Ordinarily, that'd be true. But not today.

THE CAPTAIN. Disinheriting me! My own father!

ABLE. Sad, isn't it?

THE CAPTAIN. I want proof of this!

ABLE. Take my word, sir! It's true, really!

THE CAPTAIN. Oh, no! You'll prove it! *(Hand on his sword scabbard.)* You'll prove it or I'll split you from your brow to your bunghole, understand?

ABLE. It's subtle, but I get it! *(As THE CAPTAIN chases ABLE up the stairs:)* Wait!

THE CAPTAIN. What?

ABLE. Why waste time? Why not get even? Run away from home! Join the army!

QUICK BLACKOUT

SCENE 4

(SLY's bedroom. Empty. Door down stage right opens and ABLE looks around cautiously, then beckons to THE CAPTAIN, who enters behind him.)

ABLE. Come in, come in and be quiet. Don't clank your medals! Now, behind that passageway is a door. Wait in there and you'll hear everything. We've beaten your father here, but then he moves like a snail with a hernia. *(As THE CAPTAIN starts up the stairs.)* Don't rattle your sword! Christ, you're as quiet as a battleship on tiptoe.

THE CAPTAIN. If you're hoodwinking me, you'll be a soprano by nightfall.

ABLE. For my part, I have no fear. Now, you play yours. Go!

(THE CAPTAIN EXITS, as SLY ENTERS through door Down Stage Left.)

SLY. Able! How did you do?

ABLE. A double bullseye!

SLY. Truckle *and* Crouch?

ABLE. One is bringing his will, the other his missus - both of which you can fill in at your convenience.

SLY. *(Impressed.)* How did you ever arrange it?

ABLE. Crouch is naming you his heir instead of his son to gain your favor.

SLY. Delicious! And Truckle?

ABLE. I told him that though your health had rallied you still needed massive doses of another man's wife.

SLY. My boy, you live up to every expectation!

ABLE. While they live down to theirs! *(A knock on the door Stage Right. ABLE, looking through the door's peephole, is not happy at who he sees on the other side.)* It's Truckle! *(SLY immediately begins a series of slow, Asian exercises, preparing to show how fit HE's feeling for TRUCKLE's benefit. ABLE opens the door, and an anxious TRUCKLE ENTERS.)*

TRUCKLE. Friend Sly! Your sudden attack of health comes as a terrible shock - a marvelous, terrible shock. But my wife is a very pious woman. Any talk of bed will absolutely have to be couched.

SLY. What exquisite sensitivity, sir.

TRUCKLE. Dare I ask you, sir, ill as you've been, to pretend to be sick?

SLY. Ill as I've been, it will be no trouble at all, sir. Fetch your wife. I'll decompress myself.

TRUCKLE. *(Heading for door Stage Right.)* Bless you, sir, bless you.

(He EXITS door Stage Right.)

SLY. *(Gleefully, to ABLE.)* Is he priceless? All that's left is to carve "Welcome" on his ass and unfold him on the front step. Help me! *(ABLE, preoccupied, helps tuck SLY in.)* My shawl! *(As ABLE hands it to him.)* What's the matter, Able? It's all going as planned.

ABLE. Not the way *I* planned it. Old man Crouch was supposed to come first.

SLY. *(Putting the shawl on his head.)* Oh, damn that relic!

ABLE. *(An eye toward the stairs, his mind on the Off Stage CAPTAIN.)* Sir, there's something I should tell you.

(Stage Right door opens.)

SLY. *(To ABLE.)* Later!

(TRUCKLE and MRS. TRUCKLE ENTER door Stage Right, as SLY lays back on pillows.)

TRUCKLE. Sly, it's me, Abner Truckle. I've brought my nurse to wife you.

(As the TRUCKLES cross to the bed, ABLE moves toward the stairs.)

SLY. Ah, let me see your good lady wife. Show me the lovely remedy.

TRUCKLE. This is Simplicity, sir.

SLY. Ah, one can only hope.

TRUCKLE. *(Taking MRS. TRUCKLE aside.)* Be brave, my dear. Don't be scared if he gets all fevered and starts thrashing up against you. Now, you understand why I pitied him.

MRS. TRUCKLE. Oh, I do.

TRUCKLE. *(Starting for Down Stage Right door.)* Farewell, friend

SLY FOX

Sly.

    SLY. *(Squinting.)* Is that you, Truckle? It's all so faint.
    TRUCKLE. You can make out my wife here?
    SLY. I'll certainly try, yes.

(ABLE re-enters at the top of the stairs, rubbing his buttock. Obviously HE's been kicked by the Off Stage CAPTAIN.)

    TRUCKLE. Let's go, Able. This is only for God's ears.
    ABLE. *(Muttering.)* God's and the Navy's.

(They EXIT Stage Right door. All is still a moment. Then:)

    SLY. *(To MRS. TRUCKLE.)* Your hand, my dear.

(MRS. TRUCKLE complies.)

    SLY. *(Continued.)* Oh, how it kindles me. Lovely, firm, the warmth of young blood. Like King David when he was old and cold, this comforts me in places I'd given up for lost.
    MRS. TRUCKLE. Grandmother Violet in Boston —
    SLY. *(Cuts in.)* Closer, child. There ears miss every other word. Grandmother, who, where?
    MRS. TRUCKLE. *(Closer, louder.)* Grandmother Violet in Boston, when she was aged and plagued by gout, she would lay little dogs on her legs, and it never failed to help her. Let me bring you another blanket.
    SLY. Do you really want me to get better, my dear?
    MRS. TRUCKLE. Oh, surely, sir. I'll say five Hail Marys for you and three Our Fathers.
    SLY. Forget about Marys and Fathers and covering me with puppies. I know a magic cure. It was taught me by a hundred year old Indian who dreamed it up on his wedding night.
    MRS. TRUCKLE. Truly?

SLY FOX

SLY. Put your hand here. *(He places her hand on his chest. A pause, then.)* Under here. *(Putting her hand under his nightshirt.)* Now, move it lightly and think only the kindest of thoughts.

MRS. TRUCKLE. I never heard of this.

SLY. *(Moving his hand with hers.)* It's written out on a buffalo skin. We can read it later. *(Enjoys the proceedings a moment, then.)* Ah, yes. Very good.

MRS. TRUCKLE. I'm doing it right?

SLY. Lightly, lightly. Are you thinking kind thoughts, my dear?

MRS. TRUCKLE. Thoughts of virtue, sir.

SLY. Suit yourself.

MRS. TRUCKLE. *(Surprised.)* Am I mistaken, sir?

SLY. Not yet.

MRS. TRUCKLE. You seem to be getting stronger.

SLY. Yes.

MRS. TRUCKLE. And stronger.

SLY. Yes!

(He sits straight up.)

MRS. TRUCKLE. *(Startled.)* Sir! You have risen!

SLY. Oh, let me count the ways!

MRS. TRUCKLE. It's a miracle! Madonna, a miracle!

SLY. *(Embracing her.)* You're the Madonna! When all hope was gone, you restored me!

(MRS. TRUCKLE tries to get him to lie back.)

MRS. TRUCKLE. You must thank God for this, sir.

SLY. *(Groping for her.)* You're closer!

MRS. TRUCKLE. *(Disengaging herself.)* I was only doing the Lord's work. Have care you don't chill, sir. You could easily take sick again.

SLY. Never again! Feel this hand! *(He grasps hers.)* Is it weak any-

SLY FOX

more? Cold?

MRS. TRUCKLE. It pulses with life!

SLY. These arms! *(Embraces her tightly.)* These arms could tear a woman in half - and then make love to both of them!

MRS. TRUCKLE. It's true! You have power, sir! Immense power! *(A beat, then.)* Have you a candle?

SLY. A candle? *(Intrigued.)* You want a — ?

MRS. TRUCKLE. The occasion calls for a votive offering.

SLY. *(Starting to get out of bed.)* I'm sure there must be some around here somewhere.

MRS. TRUCKLE. *(Pushing him back.)* Oh, don't get up, sir.

(As she goes to the armoire to search:)

SLY. Will nothing else do? A buggy whip perhaps?

MRS. TRUCKLE. An answered prayer must always be illuminated. The glow of a candle is a shining testament to the power of faith.

SLY. *(Starting to stand.)* My dear — *(She opens the armoire door and it hits SLY in the head, sending him nearly unconscious, back on the bed. Unaware of the damage she has done to SLY, she goes to the desk in her search for the candle. SLY, getting to the floor, follows her on his knees.)*

MRS. TRUCKLE. Grandmother Violet always had a ready supply. But then she was ever prepared to do the Lord's work. *(Seeing him on the floor behind her.)* Sir! You have fallen way out of bed! Gently, gently! You mustn't overdo the miracle! *(She kneels to help him. The result is, SLY's head somehow disappears under her skirt.)* Sir!!

(Which causes THE CAPTAIN to appear at the top of the stairs and come charging into the scene. Which, in turn, causes MRS. TRUCKLE to scream.)

THE CAPTAIN. *(Pulling SLY to his feet.)* You cad! You slimy bilge!

If I could, I would swab the deck with you! *(He delivers a blow which sends SLY sprawling back onto on the bed, and off the other side. Then, crossing to the window, he shouts out.)* Police! Police! Up here, Officer! Someone's been pawed! Someone's been raped! *(Listens, then.)* Not me! This woman! *(Turning to MRS. TRUCKLE.)* Come here!

MRS. TRUCKLE. *(Horrified.)* I'm not allowed near windows!

THE CAPTAIN. *(Out the window.)* Get up here! On the double! *(He helps MRS. TRUCKLE into a chair, as a police whistle is heard Off Stage.)* Sit, madame. Let your fears stand down.

(ABLE rushes in through Down Stage Right door, as: The whistle-blowing POLICE CHIEF rushes on through Up Stage Left door, followed by THREE POLICEMEN.)

THE CHIEF. I'm the Chief of Police! Someone called for help!

THE CAPTAIN. I want to prefer charges!

THE CHIEF. Which charges do you prefer?

THE CAPTAIN. I caught that degenerate lump lusting and fondling this poor woman, even as she was in mid-piety!

THE CHIEF. *(Crossing to her.)* Begging your forgiveness, ma'am. Given my choice of druthers, please understand I would not further burden you in this hour of your extreme disruptitude. The law, however, requires that I put all private parts of myself to one side so that I might better penetrate my understanding of what occurred during the attack against your personal body, which the alleged accused I have just come to learn was in the very act of trying to mount himself upon. *(Taking out a note pad and pencil.)* I'll want to know all the details. You might have to repeat them several times. Slowly. I'll want to know about his hot, probing hands and how you fought and scratched him, as your own breath became very hot, the both of you panting, panting heavily and how you scratched his hot face with your sharp nails, and then, your limbs entwined, you rolled across the floor, your body tumbling over his, your hot cheeks on fire —

MRS. TRUCKLE. I never did that!

THE CHIEF. *(Eagerly.)* Would you like to?

MRS. TRUCKLE. I was here to offer a prayer.

ABLE. Right! It was a little religious frenzy, that's all! Just some good natured praying.

THE CHIEF. Who're you?

THE CAPTAIN. He set the whole scene up! They both should hang!

ABLE. *(Pointing to SLY.)* See for yourself, sir. The man can't stand, let alone swing!

(TRUCKLE ENTERS Down Stage Right door, overhearing:)

THE CHIEF. *(To POLICEMEN, regarding SLY.)* Fetch his servants to carry him!

(As POLICEMEN EXIT:)

TRUCKLE. Is he dead?

MRS. TRUCKLE. Oh, Abner!

(As SHE runs into his arms:)

THE CHIEF. Are you the husband of the rapee?

TRUCKLE. The what-ee?

THE CAPTAIN. Yes, he's the husband! And he brought her here to be ravaged! I heard it all!

THE CHIEF. *(Eager once more.)* You did? Do you remember any of the words?

ABLE. *(To SLY, explaining THE CAPTAIN's presence.)* He forced his way in. He forced me to hide him!

(CROUCH ENTERS Stage Right door, waving a document.)

CROUCH. I've got it! I've got my new will! *(Seeing THE CAP-TAIN.)* Sonny boy!

THE CAPTAIN. *(Grabbing the will.)* Give me that, you old poop! *(Scanning the will.)* "Being of sound mind and body — " (to CROUCH.) If you had anything like the first, you'd know you don't have anything like the second.

(POLICEMEN re-enter with THE SERVANTS.)

THE CHIEF. *(Pointing at SLY.)* Help him up! Get him dressed! Then, everyone down to the station!

ABLE. The station! *(SLY moans, his hand going to his "pained" head.)* His head! His fevered head, sir!

THE CHIEF. Makes no never-mind! Dress him!

(As THE SERVANTS help SLY into the wheel chair, he emits a croak, clutches his heart.)

ABLE. *(Another plea to THE CHIEF.)* His heart, sir! His failing heart! His fevered head! You can't drag a man out of a warm deathbed. The man can barely walk!

THE CHIEF. Then, roll him! Let's go!

SLY. Wait! Wait! My chest!

ABLE. His chest! *(To THE CHIEF.)* Sir! His chest! He can't breathe!

SLY. No, no! This chest! *(Points to the one at the foot of his bed.)* I can't leave all I own behind!

THE CHIEF. The police'll be here to guard it.

SLY. God help me!

THE CHIEF. All right, people! Let's move!

(As SLY is wheeled toward door Down Stage Right:)

ABLE. This is murder, sir! Official murder!

SLY. I'm innocent! I'm an innocent man! If I'm not, may this entire city fall to the ground.

(The lights suddenly begin to flicker, along with a loud, ominous rumble, causing EVERYONE to lurch, even MISS FANCY, who, entering door Down Stage Right, loses her footing and falls onto SLY'S lap.)

THE CHIEF. Take him away!

CURTAIN

ACT 2

SCENE 1

(A jail cell. Dank and dirty. A dejected SLY and ABLE, the occupants. An indignant MISS FANCY, their Visitor.)

MISS FANCY. I'm wise to you now, Foxwell Sly! Flim-flammin' me, while you took your health out on other women. You didn't have to con me. I'd've understood. Turnin' me away at the door, treatin' me like poison. Hangin's too good for you.

SLY. I'd gladly settle for less. Hanging doesn't go away, you know. Once they give it to you, it's forever.

MISS FANCY. Well, I'm the one person's got your ticket out of here. All you got to do is keep that sweet promise you whispered in my ear that lovin' night you asked me to retire.

(She hands him a document.)

SLY. *(Looking at it.)* An application?

MISS FANCY. For a weddin' license. Sign it and I'll swear on the stand the only way a man sick as you could make love was to be raised and lowered on a pulley.

ABLE. An expert witness, you might say.

MISS FANCY. Top'a my field.

(A POLICEMAN appears.)

POLICEMAN. *(To MISS FANCY.)* Time's up!

MISS FANCY. *(To SLY.)* Think it over, darlin'. I'd feel a whole lot better wrapped 'round your neck than a rope.

(She EXITS with POLICEMAN.)

SLY. *(Angrily.)* Blast! Months of setting up these suckers. I was playing them like a master and this is where it ends - just because I try lifting the skirt of a dimwit who all the time thought I only wanted to conduct a morning service. *(Looking at the marriage application.)* And now this one! *(THE POLICEMAN reappears with CRAVEN, then EXITS.)* Craven! Craven! How glad I am you've come!

ABLE. *(To SLY.)* Sir! Gently, sir. *(Reminding him.)* Your sickness?

SLY. What? Oh, yes. *(Weakly, to CRAVEN, as ABLE helps him to sit on top of the cot.)* That's part of my sickness, forgetting how sick I am.

CRAVEN. Is it true, what I've heard?

ABLE. What did you hear?

CRAVEN. Crouch's son is pressing charges and Sly is headed for the gallows.

SLY. My God!

ABLE. And am I up the same creek?

CRAVEN. Who cares about you? *(Pointing at SLY.)* When he goes, I not only lose my best friend but the court could take over his entire estate.

SLY.What do I do?

CRAVEN. First thing, you need a lawyer.

SLY. You're a lawyer.

CRAVEN. Then, on to the second: my fee.

SLY. Name it!

CRAVEN. If I get you off, you declare me your sole heir.

SLY. Sole and only.

CRAVEN. Half payable the minute you get out.

ABLE. We get out. Cant' you make it "we?"

CRAVEN. Your fate is tied to his. I must see that nothing is tied to either one of you. Now, I'll have to understand the case very clearly if I'm to properly obscure it in court. What're you accused of?

ABLE. Rape.

CRAVEN. *(Surprised, to SLY.)* In your condition?

SLY. I must've been delirious.

ABLE. Can he plead self-defense?

CRAVEN. Who was the woman in question?

ABLE. Mrs. Truckle.

CRAVEN. *(In disbelief.)* Mrs. Truckle? *(Beat.)* Was anyone else in the church?

ABLE. It happened at home. You can get him off, surely, sir, with Mister Sly's money? It'd be a pretty strange court that didn't find a rich man innocent.

CRAVEN. Unfortunately, the courts have recently been plagued by a rash of honest judges.

ABLE. Have we had one appointed?

CRAVEN. I'm afraid so.

SLY. Is he tough?

CRAVEN. A holy terror! Judge Bastardson. A baptist of the first water. A man with the strength of countless convictions.

SLY. I'm finished!

CRAVEN. You try to look as poorly as you can. When you appear at the trial I want you to act as if you're pounding on death's door. If the judge has a sliver of a heart, we'll touch it. I'll hurry ahead and talk to the others. We'll want the truth in court, and that takes a lot of rehearsing.

(He EXITS.)

SLY. You think he can help?

ABLE. He's perfect. Money mad as he is, he'd defend bank robbery as a crime of passion.

SLY. *(Devoutly.)* If I get out of this alive, I'm going to be a different man.

ABLE. Oh, yes, we both will, sir.

SLY. I'll never again covet another man's gold. I'll give all my wealth to good works. I pledge it now to charity. Just let me go free and I'll give up every cent!

ABLE. You're saying just the right thing, sir.

SLY. I know, I know. Good God! I wonder what poor people use for promises?

BLACKOUT

SCENE 2

(The courtroom. In fact, a saloon with the furniture rearranged. CRAVEN ENTERS, looking for TRUCKLE. A handcuffed ABLE is brought to the defendant's table. THE CAPTAIN, MISS FANCY, THE CHIEF and THE BAILIFF ENTER. THE COURT CLERK, an ancient man, who will record the proceedings in a painfully slow hand, sits sharpening his quill with a pocket knife. THE BAILIFF straightens THE JUDGE'S papers on the small table that sits on the saloon stage and serves as the judge's bench. Spectators ENTER and seat themselves at the bar and at various benches during.)

CRAVEN. *(Spotting TRUCKLE.)* Truckle! *(Goes to TRUCKLE.)* Truckle! May I have a word?

TRUCKLE. What're you doing here? I didn't hear an ambulance.

CRAVEN. I'm representing Sly in the alleged matter of the accused assault of the woman purported to be your wife.

TRUCKLE. I don't want her name mentioned here today!

CRAVEN. How is that possible? She was the victim.

TRUCKLE. She was the victim of nothing! Nothing happened!

SLY FOX

CRAVEN. Exactly! Nothing at all.

TRUCKLE. They were praying. It was spirited! They were exalted!

CRAVEN. Right!

TRUCKLE. He probably fell up her dress!

(CRAVEN spots CROUCH entering, crosses to him.)

CRAVEN. Crouch!

CROUCH. *(Pathetically.)* Terrible day. I could lose all my money - my son.

CRAVEN. My heart goes out to you.

CROUCH. Ah, stuff your heart!

CRAVEN. I'm here to help.

CROUCH. I'm here to get some.

CRAVEN. *(His strategy.)* Sly never suggested you re-do your will. It was your idea - a joke to please a dying man.

CROUCH. A joke?

CRAVEN. You don't mind telling a little white lie?

CROUCH. Any color, I don't mind.

THE BAILIFF. *(Joining them.)* Craven, is it true? If Sly should hang, would the court get all he owns?

CRAVEN. It could happen.

TRUCKLE. Damn! I wish the law would die!

CROUCH. Die! Die!

CRAVEN. I'll do my best!

CROUCH. Or your worst!

TRUCKLE. Whatever it takes!

BAILIFF. The court will rise! His honor - the Honorable - Thunder T. Bastardson!

(ALL comply, as THE JUDGE, a no nonsense gentleman, ENTERS, takes his place on the stage and raps his gavel, which he removes from the holster on his hip.)

SLY FOX

THE JUDGE. By the power of God invested directly in me, this court is now in session!

(All sit, except CRAVEN.)

CRAVEN. Your honor!
THE JUDGE. Sit down!
CRAVEN. But I am the lawyer for the defendant.
THE JUDGE. That's your red wagon! Sit down!

(He bangs his gavel. CRAVEN sits.)

THE JUDGE. *(Continued.)* Now, we have before us a very trying case. All the way back to the biblical times of yore, rape has been one of the most heinous offenses known to man. And it can be pretty rough on women, too. *(The courtroom breaks into laughter. THE JUDGE is stern in his disapproval.)* I'm warning everybody present here that, because of the delicate nature of this charge, I won't put up with anyone sniggering so much as a titter. *(Consulting his papers.)* Do we have all the witnesses that have been cited in this, the case of the Territory versus Foxwell J. Sly and his servant, Simon Able - the second, the accomplice of the first, who is accused by Captain Luther Crouch of the alleged molefestation of Mrs. Abner Truckle?

CRAVEN. *(Rising.)* Everyone is present, your Honor, except for Mister Sly, who languishes in his cell, his life hanging by a mere thread.

THE JUDGE. I decide who hangs by what around here! *(To BAILIFF.)* Fetch the defendant!

(BAILIFF starts to EXIT, stops as:)

CRAVEN. It would be impossible for you to be impartial were you to see him, Your Magistry. His presence will move the court to tears.

His cracked, encrusted lips fairly cry out for compassion. His debilitation is exceeded only by his decrepitude.

THE CAPTAIN. *(Jumping up.)* Rot! He's getting paid by the lie!

THE JUDGE. *(Banging his gavel.)* Sit down! I object to your interruption and my objection is sustained! Sit down! Bailiff, fetch me up the prisoner.

THE BAILIFF. Yes, Your Honor.

(BAILIFF EXITS.)

THE JUDGE. Now, then, is the Chief of Police here?

THE CHIEF. *(Rising.)* I am in full attendance, Your Honor.

THE JUDGE. Then before the accused appears, why don't you search your professional memory and kindly construe up the events for us.

THE CHIEF. Yes, sir. *(On taking the stand.)* Earlier today, I and my men were on patrol, continuing our vigilant search for the "Frisco Flasher," when suddenly comes these shouts of hanky panky being committed. Well, sir, quick as a wink, we hot-footed it into the house of the alleged accused, to find Mrs. Truckle here there — *(MRS. TRUCKLE sobs into her handkerchief.)* Crying pretty much those very same tears. But on looking around there was no sex act to be seen anywhere. Which is pretty much the way my luck's been running lately.

THE CAPTAIN. It was never done, thanks to me! One crack and I laid the lecher low!

THE CHIEF. Mister Sly'd been knocked for six, Your Honor.

CRAVEN. *(Pointing at THE CAPTAIN.)* The victim of this shipload of bilge!

THE CHIEF. *(Pointing at ABLE.)* And this one was prancing about, too!

THE JUDGE. *(To ABLE.)* You got a name?

ABLE. (Rising.) Simon Able, Your Honor.

THE CAPTAIN. Sly's bootscraper, his bumwiper!

ABLE. I care for the poor, sick gentleman, Your Honor. I look after his every need.

THE CHIEF. *(To THE JUDGE.)* He tried to cover up with a lot of bugle oil, but I could tell he was trying to get us away quick.

CRAVEN. Away from a dying man's bed - highly reasonable.

THE CHIEF. Then I headed everyone for the station. *(Indicating MISS FANCY.)* Meeting this one coming in as we were going out.

THE JUDGE. *(Consults his papers.)* That would be Miss Fancy?

MISS FANCY. I'm honored to be recognized.

THE CAPTAIN. *(Sneers.)* I'm sure. *(to THE JUDGE.)* For four dollars, you can recognize her twice!

THE JUDGE. Quiet! *(Bangs his gavel, turns to THE CLERK.)* Mister Clerk, did you get all that?

THE CLERK. *(Writing.)* Some.

THE JUDGE . Well, take your time, get it right. *(Turning.)* Does all this jibe with your account so far, Captain? After all you're the accuser here.

CRAVEN. He should be the accused, if it please the court. Accused of breaking the peace! Accused of assault and battery! And quite possibly - since, as we speak, his poor victim lies heaped in a helpless lump in his cell - accused of possibly murder!

THE CAPTAIN. *(Charging at CRAVEN.)* False! False, you document-louse! You court crab!

THE JUDGE. *(Banging his gavel.)* Quiet! Quiet! *(To THE CAPTAIN.)* You offend the dignity of these chambers once more and I'll come down there and kick you where you live! Now, get on with your lies.

THE CHIEF. *(Taking the stand.)* Yes, sir.

THE JUDGE. *(To THE CHIEF, nodding at THE CAPTAIN.)* Not yours, his.

THE CHIEF. *(Getting up.)* Yes, sir.

THE CAPTAIN. *(Taking the stand.)* It all started when I paid a visit to Sly's house.

THE JUDGE. At his invitation?

THE CAPTAIN. I'd be ashamed to be invited by the likes of that swindler. I sneaked in.

CRAVEN. You hear, Your Honor? Ssssssssneaked!

THE JUDGE. *(To THE CLERK.)* Note that in the record.

THE CLERK. *(Writing laboriously.)* "Search for the 'Frisco Flasher'..."

THE JUDGE. *(To THE CAPTAIN.)* Proceed ahead, Cap'n.

THE CAPTAIN. I came secretly because that other liar over there —*(He points at ABLE.)*

CRAVEN. *(Cuts in.)* The court will observe that the witness calls everyone a swindler and a liar while only he is honorable.

THE CAPTAIN. *(Ignoring him, continuing.)* Had informed me that my father, the feeble-minded idiot, had disinherited me.

CRAVEN. His own father! Has the court ever heard such disrespect?

THE CAPTAIN. I speak the truth, Your Honor. Age has emptied his addled head. Hold my father up to your ear and you can hear the sea. Why else would he disown me? While I was hiding in Sly's house to learn why, I suddenly began to hear sounds. First, the sound of a man threatening to give a woman sexual pleasure. Then, there's a commotion; then, I hear her cry out.

CRAVEN. In her ecstasy!

MRS. TRUCKLE. *(Stands, protesting.)* I have never been in ecstasy!

TRUCKLE. (Standing.) I can vouch for that!

THE JUDGE. *(To THE CLERK.)* Did you get that?

THE CLERK. *(Writing.)* "His bootscraper, his bumwiper — "

THE JUDGE. *(To the TRUCKLES.)* Sit down, both you Truckles! *(The TRUCKLES sit.)* Captain.

THE CAPTAIN. So I bust into the room, whereupon Sly is imposing his body upon her's.

THE JUDGE. *(To MRS. TRUCKLE.)* Is this true, Madame? Did Foxwell Sly attempt to force on you was is known in the law as illegal entry?

MRS. TRUCKLE. Perhaps he mistook my humanity for actual interest. Please let me go home, Your Honor, I have suffered enough.

SLY FOX

THE JUDGE. I'm sure you have, but I'd be neglecting my duty if I didn't ask you to go on suffering just a little more for the record. *(He gestures toward the stand. MRS. TRUCKLE goes to it.)* Now, tell me: did this Sly get violent? Did he lay his hand on you?

MRS. TRUCKLE. That is difficult to answer, Your Honor.

THE JUDGE. *(Sternly.)* A man's life is in the balance, woman. I ask you again. Did Foxwell Sly touch any part of your body better left untouched?

MRS. TRUCKLE. *(Pauses, then)* I touched him first.

(Her statement stirs a murmur in the courtroom.)

THE JUDGE. *(To MRS. TRUCKLE.)* Go on.

MRS. TRUCKLE. Hoping to give him relief, I laid my hand on his heart.

THE JUDGE. How was he dressed?

MRS. TRUCKLE. He was wearing his night gown.

THE JUDGE. And you placed your hand on it.

MRS. TRUCKLE. Under.

THE JUDGE. Under the nightgown?

MRS. TRUCKLE. Under.

THE JUDGE. On his chest?

MRS. TRUCKLE. Yes.

THE JUDGE. His bare chest?

MRS. TRUCKLE. Yes, Your Honor.

THE JUDGE. With your bare fingers? Skin on skin?

MRS. TRUCKLE. Yes, sir.

THE JUDGE. Flesh on flesh.

THE CHIEF. *(Fervently.)* Come with me! Touch me! Someplace! Anyplace on my flesh!

(THE CHIEF rushes to MRS. TRUCKLE, and throws himself at her feet. Tearing his uniform top aside, he reveals only his suspenders and

his shirtless chest.)

THE JUDGE. *(Banging his gavel.)* Stop that! Stop! Stop! Stop! Stop!

(MRS. TRUCKLE screams. POLICEMEN and TRUCKLE try to restrain THE CHIEF, who suddenly stops his flashing and blows his whistle professionally.)

THE CHIEF. All right! The show's over! Let's have a little order here!

THE JUDGE. *(To THE CHIEF.)* You ought to be ashamed of yourself!

THE CHIEF. *(Remorsefully.)* I was carried away, Your Honor. My wife died yesterday and it's been hell.

THE JUDGE. Carried away, my foot! *(Bangs gavel.)* I'm fining you one month's graft. Pay the clerk before you go, you twit! *(to THE CLERK.)* Make a note of that.

THE CLERK. *(Writing, muttering.)* "Illegal entry —."

(THE CHIEF takes his seat. Order is restored.)

THE JUDGE. Mrs. Truckle, the court apologizes for the attack on you by the Chief of Police and would like to hear more of the earlier attack by Foxwell Sly.

MRS. TRUCKLE. *(Weakly.)* Yes, Your Honor.

THE JUDGE. Are you able to continue?

MRS. TRUCKLE. Do I have time for a quick Mass somewhere?

THE JUDGE. I'm afraid not. Please go on.

MRS. TRUCKLE. As I said - at Mister Sly's request - I laid my hand on his chest.

(She glances nervously at THE CHIEF.)

THE JUDGE. *(Reassuringly.)* I'm watching him.

MRS. TRUCKLE. Traced it along his body, stroking him gently, ever so gently. And that's when it happened.

THE JUDGE. What happened?

MRS. TRUCKLE. The miracle occurred!

THE JUDGE. What miracle?

MRS. TRUCKLE. *(Still amazed.)* His strength arose!!

THE JUDGE. Uh huh. *(Aside to THE CLERK.)* The woman's a bimbo. *(To MRS. TRUCKLE.)* What happened then? Did this Sly insist his body on yours? Did he force himself husband-like upon you?

MRS. TRUCKLE. A husband is different, Your Honor. A wife expects him to force himself on her. That's a good Christian marriage.

THE JUDGE. But he behaved like a animal?

MRS. TRUCKLE. Only on our wedding night. He wanted to keep a light on.

THE JUDGE. I was talking about Sly.

MRS. TRUCKLE. *(Flustered.)* Oh, please let me go home, Your Honor! My shame is unbearable!

TRUCKLE. *(Rising, taking MRS. TRUCKLE back to her seat.)* Both our shames, Your Honor. This has been a big day for us, shamefully speaking.

THE JUDGE. You must be Mister Truckle.

TRUCKLE. Yes, sir, I must. I have no other choice.

THE JUDGE. How do you come to know Foxwell Sly?

TRUCKLE. *(Taking the stand.)* I'm an accountant, sir. I mind other people's business. For some time now, I've looked after Sly's affairs.

THE JUDGE. And did it ever occur to you he might want to make out of your own wife one of them!

TRUCKLE. Never! If even then. The man is a saint. I trust him as I would my own brother. If I hadn't had only sisters. Except one was very masculine.

THE JUDGE. Mister Sly is very wealthy, is he not?

TRUCKLE. I'm sure I don't know.

THE JUDGE. Didn't you say you was his accountant?

TRUCKLE. That's right, I did. And he's very wealthy.

THE JUDGE. Were you interested in getting your hands on his money?

TRUCKLE. Most of his money I have him. What reason would I have?

THE JUDGE. To get it back!

TRUCKLE. Yes. That would be a reason.

THE JUDGE. To get your own back - and maybe a whole lot more.

TRUCKLE. *(Worried.)* What is his Honor suggesting, Your Honor?

THE JUDGE. That the Captain's charge is true! That you delivered your own wife for another man's abusement!

TRUCKLE. False!

THE CAPTAIN. *(Jumping up.)* I heard you! *(Pointing at ABLE.)* And that one arranged it!

ABLE. I did?

CRAVEN. With Truckle?

ABLE. A husband that jealous?

CRAVEN. To the point of insanity?

TRUCKLE. I am! *(Crossing to MRS. TRUCKLE.)* Tell the judge! Have I ever let another man see so much as your ankles?

MRS. TRUCKLE. *(Rises. To THE JUDGE.)* He bought me chastity shoes!

CRAVEN. *(To THE CAPTAIN.)* Now, who's the liar, you liar!

THE CAPTAIN. *(Reaching for his sword.)* Shut your cakehole or I'll cut you up for jerky!

THE JUDGE. *(Bangs gavel.)* Order! Order! Order! One more outburst, Captain, and I will hold you in even more contempt than I do now! Sit down!

THE CAPTAIN. *(Crossing to the bench.)* Your Honor, understand my anger. (Producing a document.) My father's will, signed by his own hand, cutting me off without a penny!

SLY FOX

CRAVEN. *(Whispers hoarsely.)* Mr. Crouch! You're on! Run! Run!

CROUCH. *(Hurrying to the bench.)* I can explain, Your Honor. I am Jethro Crouch.

THE JUDGE. Explain what?

CROUCH. The defendant is very dear to me.

THE CAPTAIN. Dearer than a son!

CROUCH. *(To THE CAPTAIN.)* Please! *(To no one in particular.)* The navy's made him so cranky! *(To THE JUDGE.)* That will was for Sly's benefit.

THE JUDGE. Obviously.

CROUCH. But I wasn't serious. It was meant as a joke.

THE JUDGE. A joke?

CROUCH. Yes, sir.

THE JUDGE. You find death funny?

CROUCH. Yes, sir. In the daytime.

THE JUDGE. Well, the humor of it excapes me.

ABLE. *(Approaching THE JUDGE.)* He did it to cheer Sly up, sir. To make the poor man think he'd outlived him.

CROUCH. *(To THE JUDGE.)* What he said is what I meant.

ABLE. And I in turn, Your Honor, enjoyed the little joke of fooling the Captain. I thought I'd make him jealous, let him hear it all acted out, but was all a joke, Your Honor. Honest. *(To THE CLERK.)* Put that down: "It was all a joke."

THE CLERK. *(Writing, muttering.)* "The woman's a bimbo —"

(Suddenly, ALL eyes turn, as "SLY" is wheeled in on his cell cot by THE BAILIFF and a POLICEMAN. From the look of the body, it could be a corpse.)

CRAVEN. There is the "villain," Your Honor! There is the attacker of virtue! Look at him on his - deathcot. His pulse beating from memory. Look at those pathetic, powerless hands that we are told reached out in lust toward a woman of the opposing sex!

THE CAPTAIN. We'll see how ill he is. Let me take his temperature!

(He draws his sword and makes for the cot.)

THE JUDGE. *(To POLICEMEN.)* Stop him! *(POLICEMEN restrain THE CAPTAIN.)* Somebody get his sword! *(In the commotion that ensues, THE CHIEF kneels behind MRS. TRUCKLE, opens his jacket, and exposes himself to her once more. MRS. TRUCKLE screeches. The courtroom is thrown into further pandemonium. Banging his gavel:)* Order! Stop that! This is not a saloon! Sit down! Everybody sit down - or I'll throw a noose around the place and hang the whole building! *(The room settles down. Looking at SLY:)* That is one sad lookin' critter.

THE CAPTAIN. Hardly the way he looked, Your Honor, when he tried to maul this fair woman.

THE JUDGE. I assume he was fittern' that.

(During the above, ABLE has whispered to CRAVEN.)

CRAVEN. *(Approaching THE JUDGE.)* Your Honor, the defense would like to call a surprise witness.

THE JUDGE. *(Angrily.)* Why wasn't I told this before?

CRAVEN. That would've spoiled the surprise. I call to the stand - Miss Merrilee Fancy.

BAILIFF. *(Up.)* Miss Merrilee Fancy to the stand.

(As MISS FANCY crosses to the stand, ABLE hands her the marriage application.)

MISS FANCY. *(Surprised, delighted.)* He signed it!

ABLE. Love conquers all, my dear.

CRAVEN. *(After MISS FANCY is seated.)* Miss Fancy, please, if you will, describe your occupation to the court.

MISS FANCY. I think of myself as a - pleasure engineer.

CRAVEN. Very good. And you are quite expert at what it is you do by those who are interested in having you do it to them?

MISS FANCY. The word "refund" has yet to be spoken in my presence.

CRAVEN. In your professional capacity, the condition of a - uh - "companion" - is immediately discernible to you?

MISS FANCY. Oh, yes. Right off.

CRAVEN. And the defendant was such a "companion" for some time?

MISS FANCY. As reg'lar as rain.

CRAVEN. Please tell the court of his sexual prowess from your own first-hand experience.

MISS FANCY. In the beginning, Mister Sly was very active, very strong in that respect. As his illness overtook him, though, he would tire more easily. Got so, he finally stopped tryin' altogether, and we'd just talk. Then, after awhile, he couldn't even hold up his end of a conversation. Our last nights together, I would just read to him.

CRAVEN. He never touched your body.

MISS FANCY. Only if he wanted me to turn the page.

THE JUDGE. You swear to that under oath?

MISS FANCY. *(Her best smile.)* Or under anything you like, Your Honor.

CRAVEN. Proof, Your Honor! Proof of the man's total prowess-less-ness! Foxwell J. Sly could be buried safely next to any woman!

CROUCH. *(Rising.)* He is a prince!

TRUCKLE. *(Rising.)* A king of a prince!

CRAVEN. Your Honor, I ask you: who among us has ever been so loved, by so many, so obviously?

THE JUDGE. We are ready to judge. *(He gestures MISS FANCY to leave the stand.)* You may unseat yourself.

MISS FANCY. Thank you, Your Honor.

(She returns to her bar stool. There is a hushed expectancy in the room. Then:)

THE JUDGE. The accusation against Foxwell J. Sly, lying over there as Exhibit A, was based on the statement of one and one single witness only. This testimony has been contradicted by more than several other witnesses up to and including, no less than, the put-upon woman, who accuses the accused of no unseemly conduct even though, in this connection with him, she was to find herself thereunder! Moreover, the husband of the aforesaid harbors no suspicion, nor makes the charge that any act was committed upon his wife's corpus that was in any way delecti! Finally, the court feels that the miserable condition of the accused makes the possibility of an act of sex dependent only upon an act of God! Therefore, by the power vested in me by the Lord above, and California below, I hereby find the defendant - the soon-to-be-late Foxwell J. Sly - not guilty! *(The court, but for THE CAPTAIN breaks into applause.)* Order! *(Bangs his gavel.)* Order! Simon Able!

ABLE. Your Honor?

THE JUDGE. Since you are accused of complicity in what were charged as crimes against the accused, you are equally guilty of complicity in his innocence. You are both free to go!

ABLE. Thank you, sir! Thank you!

THE JUDGE. *(Gesturing to SLY.)* Better get him home. If he don't make it, my funeral parlor's right next door.

ABLE. Yes, sir.

THE JUDGE. As for you, Captain, in the future I would warn you to think twice before hauling upright citizens like this into court.

THE CAPTAIN. *(Snorts.)* Upright!

THE JUDGE. Each one of them true and trustworthy witnesses.

THE CAPTAIN. Trustworthy witnesses?! A thieving lawyer who keeps ten percent for himself when he tells you the time? A tart off the street with a turnstile for bloomers? A husband who solicits his own spouse? Or my miserly father, who buried my mother in a fruit box? *(His scorn building.)* My word - no, my spit - is worth more than all their false testimony, their pre-arranged perjury! *(Pointing at SLY.)* He bought them all! *(Pointing at THE JUDGE.)* And probably you, as well, in the bargain!

ABLE. ("Shocked") Bought? A judge of San Francisco?

(He glances at the others, who are properly outraged, but none more than THE JUDGE.)

THE JUDGE. He's suckin' around for a noose! *(To THE CAPTAIN.)* You have slandered the witnesses, perjured the defendant and impugned this court! I sentence you to thirty days in the hole! *(Bangs gavel.)* Take him out!

THE CAPTAIN. What? I get put away and not these devils?!

THE JUDGE. Thirty days more! *(As THE CHIEF and POLICE-MEN lead THE CAPTAIN off forcibly:)* I ought to throw the book at you. By God, I will throw the book at you! *(HE picks a weighty tome and throws it at THE CAPTAIN. Then:)* Court's adjourned!

(He EXITS. ALL immediately crowd about SLY and follow his cot as it is wheeled off by POLICEMEN.)

MISS FANCY. My darlin' Sly —

CRAVEN. Did you hear my defend you? I saved your life.

CROUCH. I saved some of it, too!

TRUCKLE. It was my words saved you! I told every kind of truth!

MISS FANCY. You don't have to move. We can be married lyin' down.

MRS. TRUCKLE. With it all, how I pity the man. I will pray for him.

TRUCKLE. Don't pray so close, my dear.

(ABLE watches them go; then, turns to Audience.)

ABLE. They'll never cease to amaze me. Each had so much to gain, had the judge found us guilty as sin, as indeed we are. Each could've retrieved through the court all that Sly has pulled through their noses. Yet, each, as a witness, was as false as his smile. Any amusement they've given me is giving way to fear. Jail today, the docket. If the stakes are going to be raised this high, it's time I had more say in the game. The longer I play it this way, the longer I'm in danger. The longer I'm used as someone's pawn, the longer I could be —
THE CLERK. *(Still writing.)* "Sucking around for a noose!"

BLACKOUT

SCENE 3

(SLY's bedroom. SLY dressed in his robe, ENTERS from up stage door, carrying an empty carpetbag. ABLE ENTERS down stage right door.)

ABLE. Mister Sly, the ice we're skating on is getting thinner and thinner. *(SLY, his thoughts elsewhere, pays little attention to ABLE.)* Beholden as I am to you, I've got no say in things - but if I had my druthers, I'd stop going steady with danger. *(Impatiently.)* Mister Sly, I've got to talk to you!
SLY. Talk all you want, just pack at the same time. *(Pointing at the bag.)* My silk shirts in there. My studs and my links. And anything else that glitters.

SLY FOX

ABLE. Does this mean what I hope?

SLY. We're pulling out. Before that flock of vultures flies in for the payoff.

ABLE. *(Amused.)* And Miss Fancy produces the license.

SLY. How thoughtless of me, how terribly inconsiderate. *(Taking a document from the desk.)* I could've saved the dear woman much trouble. *(IIe hands it to ABLE, who looks it over in surprise.)*

ABLE. You've got a wife.

SLY. In Toledo.

ABLE. You never said you had one.

SLY. What's a man without a family? Especially one he can be without? *(Nods at document.)* I have no need for another license. I've bagged my legal limit. *(Ré bag.)* Put it in there.

ABLE. *(Complying.)* We really are going?

SLY. To a far better place.

ABLE. Toledo?

SLY. Are you mad? We're hopping a clipper for the other side of the world. There are diamonds under the ground in Africa, my boy, and the same fools walk the earth above.

ABLE. *(Delighted.)* Your friends'll totally unravel!

SLY. I only wish I could see their faces, but we've got to make the proverbial tracks.

ABLE. *(Starting to pack.)* Yes, sir!

SLY. *(An idea.)* Able!

ABLE. Sir?

SLY. Wait!

ABLE. What?

SLY. I can!

ABLE. Can what, sir?

SLY. I can see their faces. It's possible!

ABLE. You can go and stay at the same time?

SLY. Exactly! I'm going to give that trio of swine a parting shot right between their shifty eyes! First, summon the servants.

SLY FOX

ABLE. Our servants?

SLY. Send them out into the streets to tell everyone — *(He loves this idea.)* Oh, this is my best yet!

ABLE. Tell them what?

SLY. That I'm dead!

ABLE. Dead!

SLY. Dead! In a rigorous state of mortis!

ABLE. You're serious.

SLY. The minute my "friends" come to the house, you will read them the new, the latest, the only bona fide and official will! And all the while, I'll be hiding in my bed, watching their sorrow at my passing; watching the room flood with tears. And then, the master stroke! They find out that you're getting it all!

ABLE. Me??

SLY. They learn that I have made you my sole heir! They find out that I have given them the finger from the grave! Imagine their chagrin!

ABLE. Chagrin? They'll separate me from my ass!

SLY. *(Filling in the will.)* Never! They'll fly to their lawyers! Their lawyers'll fly to lawyers! By the time the dust settles, you and I will be at sea, dining at the captain's table by night, trolling for suckers by day. *(Regarding the will.)* Is this the only one we have?

ABLE. Yes, sir.

SLY. Better buy some more. I'm down to my last will and testament. *(He laughs, enjoying his joke; then seals the will.)* Done!

(As SLY crosses to and pulls the bell cord:)

ABLE. You're pressing our luck, Mister Sly. It's foolish to stick our necks out yet again when we could get away so clean, so easy.

SLY. And not see them squirm once more? Not see them bask in degradation one last time? *(Heading for the bed.)* The servants will be sad, of course. Their dear, departed master. People speak so well of the dead, it's a pity we're not born that way. *(He pulls the Down Stage bed curtain closed, and disappears into the bed. Then, parting the bed curtain from within.)* Able! The bag!

(ABLE gets the carpet bag, hands it to him, then pulls the curtain shut. He looks about to see if all is ready, goes to the desk and retrieves SLY's will. He has only a moment to reflects on it. Hearing footsteps Off Stage, He races to the chest at the foot of the bed and kneels at it, instantly mournful as THE SERVANTS ENTER.)

FIRST SERVANT. Able, what is it?
SECOND SERVANT. Should we send for a priest?
ABLE. One who's good at digging.
THIRD SERVANT. He's dead?
ABLE. Clean through. It was the trial that did it.
FIRST SERVANT. Poor old coot.
ABLE. Spread the word. Tell his friends. There'll be those who'll want to pay their respects. Go. *(Handing SECOND SERVANT SLY's tray full of medicines.)* Your family might like these.

(SERVANTS exeunt.)

SLY. *(Parting the bed curtains.)* You are a marvelous liar. I was ready to send myself condolences.
ABLE. No one was ever trained better.
SLY. Now, sit down and write.
ABLE. *(Going to desk.)* Right. What is it I'm?
SLY. My inventory. A list of all we're taking...
ABLE. That they think is staying!
SLY. Delicious! I can taste this. *(Hearing something Off Stage.)* Someone! Quick! Write!

(SLY ducks behind the curtains. ABLE busies himself writing.)

ABLE. "Three gold watches. One sterling silver snuff box. One English leather truss — "

(THIRD SERVANT leads CRAVEN in Down Stage Right door.)

CRAVEN. *(Triumphantly.)* Over at last!
ABLE. Well, his life is over. His death is just beginning.
CRAVEN. He did fill in the will? Lived to name his heir?
ABLE. Named him loud and clear.

(Pleased, CRAVEN crosses to the chest, as: TRUCKLE ENTERS door Down Stage Right, followed by MRS. TRUCKLE.)

TRUCKLE. Able! It's not another nap? He's really dead?
MRS. TRUCKLE. I only hope dying brought him some comfort.
ABLE. Much more than you can imagine.

(CRAVEN crosses to TRUCKLE, who is touching objects possessively.)

CRAVEN. What do you want here?
TRUCKLE. Me? What do you want?
CRAVEN. I'm here on the wings of grief. And I'll thank you to leave, and stop fingering the estate.
TRUCKLE. *(Amused.)* Me? Leave? *(Chuckles.)* That's a good one.
CRAVEN. Unless, of course, you'd like to stay as a witness.
TRUCKLE. Me? A witness? *(Laughs again.)* That's another good one, eh, Able?

(CROUCH ENTERS door Stage Right.)

CROUCH. It's all up and down the street! *(Cackles.)* I knew it! I told you I'd outlive him - and I've got hemorrhoids older'n he is. *(Correcting himself.)* Was! Was!

SLY FOX

TRUCKLE. *(To CROUCH.)* Come to buy and bargain, have you?

CRAVEN. Nothing here's for sale!

CROUCH. Me, buy? I've got all I want! The only thing I need is more? I came to hear the will! The will's the words - in there's the music!

(He raps the chest with his cane.)

TRUCKLE. Of course! The will! Able, read us the will!

CROUCH. Yes, the will!

CRAVEN. Wait! We can't read it yet.

CROUCH. Why?

TRUCKLE. Why not?

CRAVEN. *(Yanking the bell pull.)* We need a witness from the court. Everything must be done legal-like.

CROUCH. Since when?

TRUCKLE. I waited long enough.

CROUCH. Time is money!

(First servant ENTERS. ABLE turns to him.)

ABLE. Run across the road, tell the judge to come right away!

FIRST SERVANT. Right!

(First servant runs off door Stage Left. A suspicious MISS FANCY ENTERS door Stage Right.)

MISS FANCY. Able, this ain't some kind'a trick so Sly can get outta marryin' me, is it?

ABLE. Not this time, darlin'.

MISS FANCY. *(Heading for the bed.)* Let's find out a hunnerd percent. I got a surefire test for tellin' if a man's got any life in him.

SLY FOX

(She starts to pull the curtains aside.)

ABLE. *(Blocking her way.)* Wait!

CROUCH. I was nearly buried by mistake once, right in the middle of a nap. *(Lights a match.)* Maybe a match on the soles of his feet —

ABLE. *(Blowing out the match.)* Please!

TRUCKLE. *(Picking up silver letter opener.)* Safe is safe! *(Crossing to bed.)* One stab in the heart to make sure!

(The ruckus at the bed stops, as THE JUDGE enters Stage Right door with a POLICEMAN.)

THE JUDGE. Bastardson's the name, funerals is my game! *(Passing out his card.)* Combining dignity and sincerity at a price. I've buried some of the best of the west. My burials are outstanding. Many surviving families have come back for seconds.

TRUCKLE. *(Handing him the will.)* What we really want, Your Honor, is a legal unsealing of the will.

THE JUDGE. Sly's dead, is he?

ABLE. Everyone here seems to think so, yes, sir.

THE JUDGE. Better bring him in soon. They don't keep too well on these hot days.

ABLE. Yes, sir.

THE JUDGE. All right, let me have your attention. Is the death of the deceased confirmed by everyone here present?

CRAVEN. Yes!

TRUCKLE. He's dead!

CROUCH. And I'm not!

THE JUDGE. There was no doctor at the end?

ABLE. There was not.

CROUCH. No doctor.

THE JUDGE. Then the man died peaceful. *(To ABLE.)* Now, then, do you recognize this as the will of the deceased?

CRAVEN. I vouch for the document as having been written by my own hand, Your Honor, with only the name of the designated heir left blank. That you will find inserted in the handwriting of the dead man - written, of course, while aforesaid hand was still alive.

THE JUDGE. Lucky for you I went to law school, you know that? All right then, I will now break the seal. *(He does.)* And read. "I, Foxwell J. Sly, being wifeless and therefore practically childless, hereby make the following disposition of all my worldly wealth. In memory of the friendship he has always shown - his almost dog-like love and affection —"

TRUCKLE. *(Proudly, to MRS. TRUCKLE.)* Dog-like!

THE JUDGE. *(Continued.)* "And desiring to repay his devotion with a fit and proper reward, I name as my sole heir - to be the unconditional possessor of all my earthly goods and gold, my beloved companion - and faithful servant - Simon Able."

CRAVEN. *(Stunned.)* Able?! What does this mean?

TRUCKLE. Able?!

CROUCH. Able? *(Beat.)* I think I just shit!

(CRAVEN and TRUCKLE move menacingly toward ABLE.)

THE JUDGE. *(Bangs his gavel.)* Order in the bedroom! Settle down!

CROUCH. This is treachery!

TRUCKLE. *(Seizing the will.)* This document is a forged fake!

CRAVEN. I contest it!

THE JUDGE. You just said you wrote it!

CRAVEN. Well, I wrote it, but I didn't write *it*!

TRUCKLE. Something's rotten here! Sly absolutely assured me I was to inherit it all!

CROUCH. He assured me the same!

TRUCKLE. *(Gathering SLY's clothes, cushions, anything.)* No! Me! Only me!

CROUCH. Sly and I were the only me!

CRAVEN. I am the only only! I was his friend! His best friend!

CROUCH. I was a better best friend!

TRUCKLE. I was the closest! I gave him all kinds of gifts!

CROUCH. You gave him crap! I know! I sold you whatever you gave him and I only sold you crap! I gave him gold! Jewelry! A fortune. My whole fortune! I willed him everything. Disinherited my own son!

TRUCKLE. Your son! I gave him Mrs. Truckle. I gave him my own wife!

THE JUDGE. What? Is that true?

TRUCKLE. *(Not realizing the implications.)* I swear it!

THE JUDGE. But you swore the opposite in court!

TRUCKLE. *(Flustered.)* I probably didn't understand the question!

THE JUDGE. Then, you lied!

TRUCKLE. Never! I wouldn't lie under oath!

THE JUDGE. Then, you're lying now!

TRUCKLE. I'm not lying! I didn't lie! I'm just telling two different truths!

(THE JUDGE, enraged, crosses to POLICEMAN at door Down Stage Right.)

THE JUDGE. Release the Captain at once! Bring him here!

FIRST POLICEMAN. *(Salutes.)* Yes, Your Honor!

(He EXITS.)

THE JUDGE. An innocent man! A United States officer! A career patriot!

CROUCH. *(Sadly.)* My sailor boy.

THE JUDGE. *(To TRUCKLE.)* In jail because of your lies! You'll pay for this! They don't call me the hanging judge just 'cause I'm well-built!

SLY FOX

(TRUCKLE sinks to his knees. MRS. TRUCKLE kneels beside him.)

TRUCKLE. *(To MRS. TRUCKLE.)* Pray! Now pray!

THE JUDGE. *(Stepping to bed.)* As for Foxwell J. Sly, I'm going to string him up and let his corpse gulp a little wind before we plow it into Potter's Field!

TRUCKLE. *(To the bed.)* I just wish you could be alive to see yourself hang!

CRAVEN. *(Holding a match to the will.)* A little flame'll fix this up!

THE JUDGE. Hold on! *(Grabbing the will.)* By your own testimony, it's valid. Therefore, the will remains in force and the aforesaid Able over there is the one, the sole, and only heir.

TRUCKLE. Sooner the devil!

CRAVEN. He rigged it in his favor!

CROUCH. It belongs to no one!

THE JUDGE. Well, if the estate's an orphan, the court'll find a good home for it.

ABLE. Your Honor, if I may say a word? The dying word of Foxwell Sly? "Give back all I stole from my friends," he said. "Beg them to forgive me so I can face them when we meet once more. I make you my heir so that you can give back all that I swindled them out of." I made a deathbed promise. Only as his heir can I keep that sacred vow.

CROUCH. You'll give back all my money? The ring?

ABLE. I'll slip it on you myself!

TRUCKLE. All I gave?

ABLE. In full and more - if I'm the heir!

TRUCKLE. But you are! No one disputes it!

CROUCH. The will is perfectly legal!

CRAVEN. A hundred percent! I wrote it myself!

THE JUDGE. Then no one objects to the disposition of the estate?

ABLE. Of course, we could always give the money to the poor —

MRS. TRUCKLE. Oh, bless you, sir!

CRAVEN. *(Outraged.)* The poor?

CROUCH. They're the worst people to give money to!
TRUCKLE. They have no experience with it at all!
ABLE. That's true.
THE JUDGE. *(To ABLE.)* Then the court'll validate the parchment.

(He starts for door Stage Right.)

ABLE. Just one request, sir? Spare Sly's remains any dishonor. The miserable soul repented and I'll be making good for him. Let me just take the body away and bury it. Nothing fancy. No box, even. A shallow hole. Sitting up, if you like.
THE JUDGE. You're a good soul! You can throw the stiff in the bay for all I care!

(He EXITS door Down Stage Right.)

ABLE. *(Calling after him.)* Good thought, sir. I'll put a heavy rock in his robe.
MISS FANCY. *(Sidling up to ABLE.)* You'll be lonely without him, but I will comfort you.
ABLE. We can start mourning first thing tonight.
MISS FANCY. *(Kissing his cheek.)* Sweet boy!

(THE CAPTAIN bursts in door Down Stage Right, in a soiled prison uniform, carrying a prison utensil.)

THE CAPTAIN. *(Enraged.)* Where is he? Where?
CRAVEN. Too late, Captain. The Judge of the Highest District has taken him.
THE CAPTAIN. Dead? Dead is he? No matter! I'll flay him like a maypole! I'll chop him so fine, he can be buried on a biscuit!

(He starts for the bed. MRS. TRUCKLE blocks his way.)

MRS. TRUCKLE. Sir, he has been punished quite enough.

THE CAPTAIN. He has? I have just been released from a cell fetid beyond belief! Roaches waited in line to bite me! My first meal crawled onto my spoon! I, just a few acts away from being declared a national hero, was forced to share quarters with a pimp, a pervert and a male molester!

ABLE. My dear sir, let my servants launch you into a hot bath. Sit and steam. Rest up for Sly's funeral. *(Expansively.)* Miss Fancy, lead the Captain to the tub. Draw the water. *(MISS FANCY escorts THE CAPTAIN to Down left Stage door.)* Warm and soothing.

MISS FANCY. I'll dip my hand in once in a while - just to make sure.

ABLE. *(Overlapping.)* Just to make sure, yes. *(MISS FANCY and THE CAPTAIN EXIT.)* And now, let me invite you all to the farewell feast of Foxwell J. Sly! A real send-off for the man we all agree died for the best - ours! We'll wine and dine and laugh at all the misers and misfits who are always losing what they have by forever wanting what they don't. Shall we say eight o'clock? Nothing's too good for my friends — make it eight-thirty!

CROUCH. My boy, naming you heir was the best thing Sly ever did!

CRAVEN. Next to actually dying.

TRUCKLE. I always pitied you for having to lick his boots.

(He kisses ABLE's hand.)

ABLE. Well, he who licks last. Now, let me see each of you later in your best and finest. There'll be music and singing and girls in black silk stockings to remind us of our grief! Tonight!

TRUCKLE. Tonight!

CROUCH. Tonight!

SLY FOX

(ALL but ABLE exeunt door Down Stage Right. The bed curtains part and SLY steps out.)

SLY. You were brilliant! It was all I could do not to applaud. One or two small criticisms, but we can discuss those on the way to the wharf. I've got a carriage 'round the back. You know, that's twice today I've tweaked that judge. I may just be ready to take on the Supreme Court. *(Pointing at the carpetbag.)* Let's be sure to take the silver service, but we'll want to travel light.

ABLE. The lighter, the better, yes, sir.

SLY. *(Handing him CRAVEN's goblet.)* And be sure to leave room for this little beauty.

ABLE. No, no, I don't think so.

SLY. Pardon?

ABLE. The goblet's part of the estate. It cannot be removed.

SLY. Very amusing. Remind me to laugh on the boat. *(Checking his pocket watch.)* Come now, boy, it's time to move.

ABLE. Move if you like, sir. But I'm not leaving my house.

SLY. *(A beat, then.)* Your house?

ABLE. And all that's in it. As you heard at the reading of the will. Along with the witnesses. And his Honor.

SLY. I see. You figure I did myself in.

ABLE. Who else but you could've out-foxed you?

SLY. *(A beat, then.)* Of course. *(Crossing to desk.)* The I.O.U.'s. They're yours. *(Offering them.)* You're free. Better'n that, we're part-ners. Fifty-fifty! Half of everything I own is yours.

ABLE. Sir, you haven't got anything left to give half away of.

SLY. *(Coolly.)* It won't work, Able.

ABLE. What can you do? Haul me into court? If that judge you double-tweaked today finds out you're still alive, he'll sentence you to life in front of a firing squad. No, sir, I'm afraid that out of the mob of sole and only heirs, I am far and away the sole and onliest.

SLY. *(Sadly.)* The son I never had.

ABLE. You taught me well. Not just a little proud of me?

SLY. Maybe. In time.

ABLE. For your own safety, sir - Miss Fancy can't keep swabbing the Captain's deck forever.

SLY. What? Oh, yes, of course. Well, I'll leave you to it - having left it to you.

(He starts for Down Stage Right door.)

ABLE. Good luck, sir.

SLY. The same to you. Whoever you do next. *(Beat.)* We had some good times.

ABLE. We had some great times.

(And they recall them fondly:)

SLY. The widow with the wooden leg.

ABLE. You jilting her left her hopping mad. *(They both laugh, then:)* Getting the money belt off the midget.

SLY. Dangling him by his ankles, to shake out all the small change. *(A beat, then.)* Beatrice and Bonnie.

ABLE. The identical twins.

SLY. Except one had a mole.

ABLE. *(Puzzled.)* I thought they both had a mole.

SLY. That's because you had the same one twice.

ABLE. *(Amused, knowing that had to be SLY's doing.)* I never once suspected.

SLY. Ah. Then - as now - that is the name of the game.

ABLE. *(Appreciatively.)* You were the best.

SLY. The tense of that remark has not gone unnoticed.

ABLE. I'm sorry, sir.

SLY. *(Starting to leave.)* Of course, of course.

ABLE. And mostly about the chest.

SLY FOX

SLY. *(At the door.)* The chest? *(Grandly.)* There are chests all over the world waiting to be filled!

(He EXITS door Down Stage Right, closing it behind him. ABLE savors his moment of triumph. He kisses the gold goblet. He tears up the I.O.U.'s., watches the pieces flutter to the floor. His eye finally falls on the chest. He crosses to it, pauses a breathless moment, and then opens the grand prize. The chest is empty. All is quiet a for a short eternity, and then: SLY re-enters through Up Stage Right door, dressed in a fur-collared topcoat, and a wonderful hat.)

SLY. There's only one way to take it all with you, my boy. *(Pointing with his cane.)* Send it on ahead.

CURTAIN

PROPERTY LIST

Act One, Scene 1
Act One—Pre Set
  On Bed
    Sheets
    Pillow
    Blanket
    Shawl
  Stage left Chest
    Coins
    Plates (gold)
  D. s. night table
    Medicine tray inside
    Mirror and Comb in top drawer
  Stool—U. s. of bed
  Center Table with
    Newspaper
    Coffee cup
    Ledger
    Inkwell & quill
    Matches
    Humidor with Cigars
    Sealing Wax
    Sealing Lamp
    Sealing Stamp
    Letter opener
    IN DRAWER—Receipts, Will, Chits, Marriage
      license
    Chinese Gong
  Chair—behind table
  Arm chair—left of center
  Chinese cupboard with

PROPERTY LIST

2 Decanters with wine
2 Wine glasses
Key ring—in Sly's robe
IN CLOSET
  Sly's robe
  Whisk broom
  Carpet bag
  Overcoat (Cape)
Hanging mirror U. L.

Stage Right
  Sheets
  Pillows
  Breakfast tray with Croissant
  Will (Craven)
  Briefcase with Will
    Goblet (gold)
  Cane
  Large diamond ring (Crouch)
  Small bottle (Truckle)
  Small bag gold dust
  Handkerchief (Truckle)
  Coin (Crouch)
  Pad and Pencil (Able)
  Room scenter
  Piece of bread
  Small box matches
  Purse (Fancy) with Marriage certificate
  Watch (Able)
  Door knock
  Act One, Scene 2—none
  Act One, Scene 3
  Eye glasses (Crouch)
  Magnifying glass on string
  Diamond ring (Fancy)
  Medallion on Gold chain

PROPERTY LIST

Sword
Act One, Scene 4
Small Bible
Will (Crouch)
2 Police clubs
Police whistle on chain
Act Two, Scene 1
Marriage certificate in Purse (Fancy)
Act Two, Scene 2
Gavel
Bible
Pen knife
Marriage certificate (Able)
Act Two, Scene 3
Gavel
Business cards (Judge)
Dagger, or pipe

Stage Left
Act Two, Scene 2
Inkwell
Ledger
Rolling cot
Blanket on cot
Will (Captain)

Act One, Pre-Set—
On Turntable
Truckle House
Small arm chair
Embroidery Frame
Fireplace Irons
Needle and Yarn (On embroidery stand)
Crucifix (Hung over mantle)
Bible, on mantle
Small Bible, on window seat

PROPERTY LIST

Crouch Office
  Desk and chair with
    Ledgers
    Inkwell & quill
    Green felt
    Paper props
  Settee

Act Two—
  Jail Cell
    Cot (without wheels)
  Court Room (Bar)
    Judge's table & chair
    on Table
      Law book
      Papers
      List of Allegations
    Spitoon next to Judge (D. S.)
    Witness chair
  On Stage Left Bar
    2 Benches
    4 Bar stools

Stage Right
  Bed sheet
  Briefcase with Gold goblet covered with velvet bag
  Blue will (Craven)
  Small bag of gold dust
  Coins for Craven & Crouch
  Piece of bread
  Door bell
  Green Will (Crouch)
  Nasal sprayer
  Whistle

PROPERTY LIST

Act Two, Scene 1
Handcuffs
Marriage certificate

Personal
Cane (Crouch)
Diamond Ring (Crouch)
Small bottle (Truckle)
Purse with Marriage certificate (Fancy)
Diamond ring (Fancy)
Magnifying glass on string (Crouch)
Eye Glasses (Crouch)
Medallion on gold chain (Fancy)
Sword (Captain)
Small Bible (Mrs. Truckle)
2 Police clubs (Policemen)
Police whistle (Police Chief)
Pen knife (Clerk)
Business cards (Judge)
Gavel (Judge)
Shawl (Sly)

Stage Left
Inkwell (Clerk)
Quill pen
Ledger
Rolling cot with blanket
Breakfast tray with
    Silver Coffee Pot
    China cup and saucer
    Saucer with slice of bread
Cane (Sly)
Large sprayer
Small sprayer
Carpet bag
Empty whiskey bottle

PROPERTY LIST

Tray with glass of brandy
Small down feather
Cream pitcher ½ full of water

On Bar
  Porcelain pot with
    wet towel
    tools
  3 Pillows

At Intermission
  Set Sly table dressing on s. L. prop table
    Humidor with
      Silver and glass oil lamp
      Initial Stamp
      Sealing wax stick
      Matches
    Ledger with
      Letter opener
      Inkwell & quill

Act One, Pre-Set
On Bed
  Sheets
  3 pillows
  Blanket
Tab bed curtains
Shutters closed
Chest
  Coins
  Gold plates
  Brass scallop shell with coins D. S. corner
D. S. *Night Table*
  Medicine tray (inside)
  Set of keys (on top)
Stool U. S. *of bed (off platform)*
U. S. *Night Table*
  Fan

PROPERTY LIST

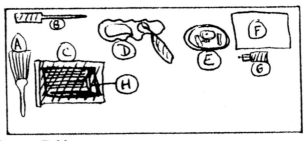

Center Table
A. Whisk broom
B. Letter opener
C. Ledger
D. Inkwell & quill
E. Sealing lamp
    In u. s. *Drawer*
      Will
      Marriage License
      Receipts
    In d. s. *Drawer*
      Duplicates
Chair behind table
Arm chair (between bed and table)
Robe on bed with keys in pocket
Chinese cupboard with
    Decanter filled with grape juice
    2 wine glasses
In closet
    Overcoat
    Clothes (dressing)
      At Top
        Both doors open
        Drawer open

E. Sealing wax
E. Sealing stamp
F. Humidor
G. Matches
H. Shirts on ledger

Pre-Set
Act One, On Turntable
  Truckle House

PROPERTY LIST

Small side chair
Embroidery Stand
Fireplace Irons
Needle and yarn (on embroidery stand)
Crucifix (Hanging over mantle)
Broom behind blue door curtain
2 pictures of Madonna over each doorway
Curtains closed
Window open
2 votive lights on mantle
Small potted fern
Portrait of Virgin over mantle
Large plaster Virgin on mantle
2 small plaster Virgins on wall either side of
    mantle
  Crouch Office
  Desk with
    Ledger
    Inkwell & quill
    Green felt (with glue)
    High backed stool
    Settee (s. l.)
    Pile of garbage

Act Two
Jail
  Cot (without wheels)
    with Blanket
    Pot
    Pillow
Courtroom
  Judge's table with chair
  Law book
  Papers
  List of allegations
  Clerk stool
  Spitoon

PROPERTY LIST

Witness chair
Gavel (on desk)

On Stage Left Bar
2 Benches
4 Bar stools

Prop Moves
During Act One, Scene 3
Strike Crouch set-up
During Act One, Scene 4
Strike Crouch set-up

Intermission
Strike table plate
Cover desk with cloth
Strike broken bannister
Strike coins & Plates from Chest
Strike Sly desk props to s. l. prop table
Close up-stage window
Test-lamp
Goblet to cupboard (wash first)
Glass under bed to cupboard (wash first)
Sly Shawl on chest
Strike stool
Strike hanky
Remove breakfast tray
Un-tab curtains
Strike bolsters
Un-do velcro

Stage Left
Act Two, Scene 2
Push bed closer to entrance
Receive and strike bed

Act Two, Scene 3
Raise and lower bed blacks
Hand Sly carpet bag
Take carpet bag from Sly

COSTUME PLOT

FOXWELL J. SLY & JUDGE—
  Night Gowns & Slippers, Night Cap, Shawl
  (2) Pair Charcoal Stripe pants
  Three Quarter Coat, Black Coat with fur collar
  Black & Red Vest, Black Hat & String Tie & Brown
      Hat & Bow Tie
  Velvet Green Robe
  Coolie Wine Robe & Straw Hat
  Off-white Shirts, Underwear
  Wellington Boots

ABLE—
  Pair Herring Bone Pants
  Black & Red Vest, Bow Tie
  Greenish-brown 3 Quarter Coat & Brown Hat
  Stripe Apron
  Wellington Boots

CRAVEN—
  Black Stripe Pants & Vest
  Black 3 Quarter Coat & Top Hat
  Grey Gloves & Cravat
  Wellington Boots

CROUCH—
  Brown Pin-stripe Pants
  Brown Vest & Tie
  Brown 3 Quarter Coat
  Brown Coat with Fur Collar & Hat
  Wine Cap, Red Shawl
  Brown Boots

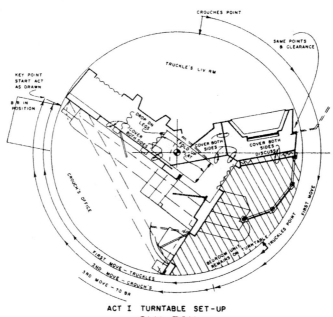

CROUCHES POINT

SAME POINTS & CLEARANCE

TRUCKLE'S LIV RM

KEY POINT
START ACT
AS DRAWN

B/R IN
POSITION

DROP DN
LEGS

COVER
BOTH SIDES

FOLD UP
FLAT

COVER BOTH
SIDES

COVER BOTH
SIDES
DISCUSS

CROUCH'S OFFICE

BEDROOM UNIT
REMAINS ON TURNTABLE

TRUCKLES POINT

FIRST MOVE

FIRST MOVE - TRUCKLES

2ND MOVE - CROUCH'S

3RD MOVE - TO B/R

ACT I TURNTABLE SET-UP
SLY FOX

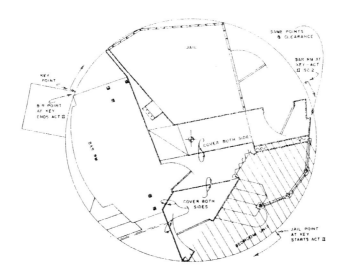

ACT II TURNTABLE SET-UP
SLY FOX

OTHER TITLES AVAILABLE FROM SAMUEL FRENCH

DEAD CITY
Sheila Callaghan

Full Length / Comic Drama / 3m, 4f / Unit Set

It's June 16, 2004. Samantha Blossom, a chipper woman in her 40s, wakes up one June morning in her Upper East Side apartment to find her life being narrated over the airwaves of public radio. She discovers in the mail an envelope addressed to her husband from his lover, which spins her raw and untethered into an odyssey through the city... a day full of chance encounters, coincidences, a quick love affair, and a fixation on the mysterious Jewel Jupiter. Jewel, the young but damaged poet genius, eventually takes a shine to Samantha and brings her on a midnight tour of the meat-packing district which changes Samantha's life forever—or doesn't. This 90 minute comic drama is a modernized, gender-reversed, relocated, hyper-theatrical riff on the novel Ulysses, occurring exactly 100 years to the day after Joyce's jaunt through Dublin.

"Wonderful... Sheila Callaghan's pleasingly witty and theatrical new drama that is a love letter to New York masquerading as hate mail... [Callaghan] writes with a world-weary tone and has a poet's gift for economical description.
The entire dead city comes alive..."
- *New York Times*

"*Dead City*, Sheila Callaghan's riff on James Joyce's Ulysses is stylish, lyrical, fascinating, occasionally irritating, and eminently worthwhile... the kind of work that is thoroughly invigorating."
- *Backstage*

SAMUELFRENCH.COM